# CALL THE DOC

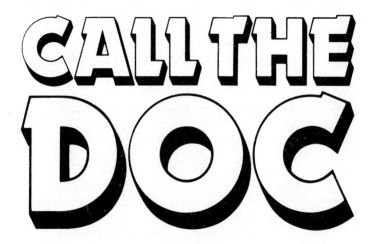

# CALL THE DOC

## Tommy Docherty

with the assistance of
Derek Henderson

Hamlyn
London · New York · Sydney · Toronto

*Acknowledgement*
The pictures on the jacket were supplied by
Colorsport (front) and Sporting Pictures (UK) Ltd (back)

Published 1981 by
The Hamlyn Publishing Group Limited
London · New York · Sydney · Toronto
Astronaut House, Feltham, Middlesex, England

ISBN 0 600 34672 2

Printed in Great Britain by
Fakenham Press Limited
Fakenham, Norfolk

*Publisher's Note*

Tommy Docherty has been connected with all aspects of professional football for
over 34 years. He has played for clubs both North and South of the Border and
was a Scottish International in the 1950s with 25 appearances for his country.
As a manager his name has been connected with some of the most celebrated
clubs in Great Britain.

He has had numerous successes, culminating in Manchester United's FA Cup
victory under his management in 1977. He has also had many disasters:
relegation, quarrels with players and various chairmen, sackings – and, finally,
the libel action which led directly to his being charged and acquitted of perjury.
Docherty's views and ideas are forcibly expressed and often controversial. While
we owed it to those he seeks to criticise to check the facts as far as was at all
possible, we are confident that they and all others referred to in this book will
come to share the view that throughout his connection with football, however
misguided or outrageous he may at times have seemed to some, 'The Doc's' sole
concern was the welfare of the game and the successful future of all those
connected with it.

# Contents

# Foreword
## *Lawrie McMenemy*

FOR SOCCER MANAGERS, life is a question of survival, and Tommy Docherty is certainly one of the great survivors. He comes from the sort of background where it was essential to be a scrapper and it's in his nature. Tommy has always jumped in where angels fear to tread, but to those who criticise him, I would say this: wasn't there something in the Bible about casting the first stone?

He'll come up with such quotes as his famous one about the Press: 'There's a place for them – but they haven't dug it yet,' and the one about directors: 'The ideal set-up is to have three – two dead and one dying.' But these are throw-away lines and typical of him. He doesn't mean any malice by them, in fact Tommy's a long way short of being as bad as he is often painted.

Like another outspoken sportsman, Freddie Trueman, he's often mis-quoted, as are all who are always ready with a comment. That's why the Press lads love him. They know if they hang round long enough, they'll get a story.

Tommy knows as I do that as a manager you don't only have to win trophies to be successful. The biggest things are getting the best out of what you have got, and giving the public what it wants. In this respect, he has nearly always succeeded.

There are some things Tommy's done which I certainly didn't approve of, but nobody can deny that he makes an impact: he lifts clubs, he increases gates, and he gets his teams on to the sports pages.

He cuts corners and he speaks his mind. But how many managers having lost the Cup Final would have rung up the opposing manager the same evening and said: 'Well done – enjoy yourselves.'

That's what he did after we had beaten Manchester United and I'll never forget it.

*September 1981*

# Prologue
## *Derek Henderson*

FOOTBALL, Tommy Docherty told me in the summer of 1981, is 'a nice, incurable disease.' It is a malady from which he will never recover, nor indeed will ever want to.

What sort of man is this son of Glasgow, whose life has seemingly been a succession of highs and lows, dotted here and there with turbulent passages?

The average fan's impression has, down the years, been fashioned—and for the most part, sullied—through a series of eye-catching and sometimes lurid newspaper headlines. But is this a reflection of the true Docherty?

I had wanted for some time to assist in putting his extraordinary story into book form but it was not until he was coaching the Australian club Sydney Olympic in the winter of 1980-81 that he said 'Okay—we'll do it.'

But I freely admit that although as a football writer I had known him in a professional capacity for a number of years, it wasn't until we immersed ourselves in preparing this story late in the summer, that I fully realised that there was much, much more to Tommy Docherty than all those clippings which occupy so much space in newspaper libraries up and down the land.

It was the lyrics of Lennon and McCartney which so wisely observed that 'life is very short, and there's no time for fussing, and fighting, my friends' and indeed Tommy's existence, on the face of it, would appear to be an attempted contradiction of that sentiment.

Docherty is colourful, controversial and even slightly eccentric in the footballing sense. He is certainly no saint. He has often done foolish, headstrong things and hated himself for them later. But I believe he has never set out deliberately to damage anyone—even those who have no time for him.

He has variously been described as a martinet, a bully, a dictator, a stormy petrel and a likeable rogue. Yet Ken Shellito, his No. 2 at Preston who has known him for 20 years, says: 'A part of him has never grown up. Yet he is one of the kindest, most warm-hearted men I know.'

Tommy's story is no mere chronicle of matches and managerial chit-chat. It is the frankly delivered story of someone who has never shirked from speaking his mind, even if the words hurt.

Naturally he has had his troubles, the most publicised being perhaps the charge of perjury, for which he stood trial and was cleared in October 1981.

We decided to begin his story at this point, and then to describe the people and events connected with Tommy's spell at Manchester United, from which the trouble arose. This seemed a better way of presenting the essential Docherty than the more straightforward chronological account.

For the convenience of readers, a 'Docherty dateline', giving the dates of Tommy's movements from club to club, is included at the back of the book.

Docherty is essentially a man of the people. I witnessed part of the reception he received from the ordinary folk on his return to Preston—and it had to be seen to be believed. Whatever his transgressions, Mr Everyman does not hold them against him—rather, I am sure, does he feel he has often been the victim of circumstance as much as being his own worst enemy.

Although this is his own story—typically abrasive, open and sometimes delightfully amusing, there are tales about himself that no man would relate in an autobiography.

Like the time he told a young injured player to borrow his Mercedes, and then took a tedious ride home himself on the underground. And about the time, for instance, when he handed over the £1,000 cheque he won for being manager of the Year to a nun, so that some spastic children could go to Lourdes. Or the time when he took Old Trafford's oldest cleaner out to a champagne lunch on her birthday . . .

This is the Doc you don't read about in the newspapers—the man whose very honesty and openness in talking to the members of my business has often been his undoing.

He has always been suspicious of quiet men, which is his way, and maybe why he is so often in the news.

Whatever their faults, the game needs the Dochertys, the Allisons and the Cloughs, however much they rile dull authority. Football must have men of their intensity of passion and purpose, otherwise it would wither.

I've a feeling there's plenty of life (and who knows, even a little more controversy) left in the Doc. Rock on, Tommy!

*Westward Ho, Devon*
*October 1981*

# 1
# Drama in Court

Tommy Docherty was cleared by a jury at the Old Bailey yesterday of two counts of perjury by unanimous verdicts after a retirement of just under two hours.

Docherty, 53, manager of Preston North End, was discharged from the dock by Judge Charles Lawson.

Docherty had denied the two offences of perjury allegedly committed while he was giving evidence in his libel action against former Manchester United footballer Willie Morgan and Granada Television at the High Court in 1978.

(The Daily Telegraph, *Wednesday, 21 October 1981*)

WHEN I STOOD in the dock and heard the foreman of the jury twice utter the words I had prayed for so long and so hard to hear – 'Not guilty' – I was crying. It was something I had not done very often in my life.

It was all over. The ordeal which both myself and Mary Brown had faced was finally at an end and I still can't quite believe it.

Nobody who has not had a serious charge hanging over his head knows quite what it is like. It's akin to someone putting a detonator to a bomb to go off at a particular time in your life, and you are living through the count down.

The crazy thing is that all along I knew I was not guilty. I kept asking myself 'What the hell am I doing here?' – and coming back to the stark reality of it all, having to accept that I *was* there – and it wasn't a nightmare. It was really frightening.

When I look back now the whole thing seemed to be running on and on like the famous 'Mousetrap'. But believe me it wasn't funny. My sense of relief at the verdict was overwhelming because there is always that nagging fear at the back of your mind that things will go against you.

Those seven days back at the Old Bailey were very much ones of mixed emotion. Even though I felt that I didn't deserve to be in the dock I felt humiliation on behalf of my family and friends.

Football has been my whole life. I had been to speak at Trevor Cherry's testimonial dinner on the Sunday—only a few hours before I was in London for the first day of the perjury hearing—but football seemed a million miles away over those few days when I felt I was fighting for my life and my reputation.

I looked round the courtroom and felt the sheer weight of the solemnity of it all. I had seen it all before but it is something you never really get used to. The jury is sworn in. All the papers are brought in. It's like being in a bull ring with everybody staring at you. It was the Queen versus Tommy Docherty. I was sitting between two prison officers in the dock, not a very comfortable feeling.

But I had the marvellous good fortune to be represented by a man whom I believe is the top Q.C., Richard du Cann, and his able junior, Mr Barry Singleton. I also thought prosecuting council, Mr Paul Purnell, was very fair.

Now and then I found myself in a little ante-room or out in the corridors mingling with defendants in other cases who were facing charges even more serious. This added to my bewilderment as to what I was doing there. If I had problems, they certainly had more...

When a case seems to swing back and forth the mind plays strange tricks. One minute I would be listening to my counsel and I'd convince myself we'd got to win. Then I would be listening to the judge's words and I'd think 'no, we've lost'.

Funny things came into my mind. I kept dwelling on silly trivial matters like: If the case went against me, I hadn't brought my shaving gear, or when would I see the kids next, or how would Mary get back home after the case?

Then suddenly it was all over and I was cleared. Compared to the dignified beginning it was a hectic finish. One of the young warders who had been sitting with me—he was a nice lad from

Oldham—practically threw me out of the dock as if to say 'Away you go.'

I'd often looked around the court at the press benches and the public gallery, where there were even people wearing the red and white scarves of Manchester United—absolutely unbelievable.

Now all I could think of was Mary, who had been like a rock for so many long months as she had stood by me, and of my friends who stuck it out with me.

When I looked back a few days later at all the trauma, and still pinching myself to believe that the cloud had been lifted from me, I asked myself what I had learned from all of it.

Two things, I think, above all. One is that it has brought me even closer to the public—the men and women in the street. They had been wonderful to me through it all. I know some of them think I have been a fool, but against that I knew that many of them who had reservations about me before figure now that I may not be such a bad chap after all.

The second is that these two costly and worrying court cases have taught me that I must put myself above any form of criticism in future and learn to take it, just as I dish it out.

My gratitude to my two counsel and my solicitor is undying. As I saw them walking along the corridor one day so deep in thought that they didn't even see me I said to myself 'If only I could have professional footballers who were equally dedicated and immersed in their work as these men—what gems I would have under me.'

The few hours after the case ended was a whirlwind. The congratulations came in from everywhere, including one from my old QPR chairman, Jim Gregory. The media people must have been surprised at my silence, but this was because I was contracted to tell my story to the *Sunday People*.

Even so the next day I read in some newspapers what I'd said after the case and what Mary had said. The strange thing was that we had spoken to nobody—and there it was in print—supposedly what we had both said.

So it was back to reality for me again. I had a job to resume at a club where everyone has been so understanding towards me.

Within a few hours I was with Preston North End on the long journey down to Devon where we lost a seven-goal thriller at Exeter, and I was back in a familiar situation–having to pick up my team and do the job I am best at.

But there was still time on the journey home on the coach that night to sit back and reflect on how the court trauma had started.

When I look back at the root of the whole Willie Morgan saga, I cannot help feeling that fate often turns on the smallest of incidents–and this was a classic example of that.

In this instance, it all began with an innocuous accident in a tennis match. It was the early summer of 1974 and I was in Spain for a fortnight's holiday when I received news that Willie had badly injured an eye during a tennis game, and there was a danger that he might lose the sight of this eye.

Without hesitation, I cut short my holiday, but to everyone's relief, the operation on his eye proved successful, though they told him he might get problems with his sight later on.

Willie missed pre-season training while recuperating, though he played in a friendly against Hull City, and in terms of fitness, did extremely well. But though he played about 30 games in the first team that season, he never found his true form, and I mentally put it down to the fact that he might not have been seeing the ball as well as before, as a result of the eye injury.

In the meantime, I had signed Steve Coppell from Tranmere with the aim of him taking over eventually from Willie a year or two hence. But Steve had been doing so well, and Willie so indifferently, that I had to leave Willie out of the side. Unfortunately Willie is the sort of player–and there are plenty of them–who takes things like this badly.

Even as a substitute, he wouldn't go out on the field and kick around with the team–he would only be interested in sitting on the bench. In my view, he went a little bit sour.

He was club captain at the time, but it was nevertheless a surprise to me when he asked for a transfer. I tried to dissuade him because I knew he had a testimonial coming up in a couple of years or so. Though he was not particularly a popular chap with some of the players–for he was one of the old brigade from Sir

Matt Busby's time – he was certainly popular with the spectators.

But he was adamant. I put it to the board and they agreed he should be put on the list. To illustrate how seriously Willie viewed the whole business of him being replaced in the team, I should say that he wanted originally to include his solicitor in the discussions about where he stood. I wouldn't have this at any price – I told him 'I'll talk things over with you – but I'm not going to have your solicitor present.'

When I told Willie the club would ask only £30,000 for him, he said he was delighted and it was a marvellous gesture. He knew that this relatively small fee would enable him to negotiate a much better personal contract.

I knew that Willie himself felt he was worth around £125,000 – though how he arrived at that valuation, I can't figure out, for he'd played seven years at Old Trafford, and the eye injury must have reduced his value.

Anyway, while we were on an Australian tour in the summer of 1975, Burnley signed Willie. Unfortunately for him, he was a flop at Turf Moor, as I think he will agree, and Burnley later transferred him to Bolton where he had a much better spell.

Things started to develop when I arrived home one night in January 1977 to discover that Willie had been sounding off on the Granada TV sports programme 'Kick Off'. I didn't see it myself that evening but I was soon told that he had said I was the worst manager he had ever served under.

I suspected at the time that the interviewer Gerald Sinstadt had prodded Willie into his comments, but nevertheless I considered that Willie was experienced enough, if he had wanted to, to shy clear of the issue.

It had always been my attitude that if someone wants to criticise one, it's their opinion, and they're entitled to it. Therefore, I had never really taken offence at anything similar before. But when a friend of mine played back the programme to me on video, I thought 'That's a bit naughty.'

I wrote asking Willie for an apology, but he declined. Up to that point I had no notion of taking the thing to court.

However, one or two people – including a well-known solicitor who was a keen supporter of United—said to me that the remarks were libellous, and that the best way to clear my name would be to go to court.

As a result, I went down to London to see the legal people who felt that I would have a great chance of a successful action.

People have since often asked me: 'Do you think you were badly advised at the time?' It's always easy to be wise after any event, but in retrospect I must concede that, judging by the way the case went, possibly I was.

It was certainly the biggest mistake of my life. I should have done exactly what I had done dozens of times previously whenever anyone had had a go at me: taken it and said nothing. But, as the saying goes, it seemed right at the time.

I'm told from a very reliable source—and I believe it—that a top counsel in Manchester offered the opinion that we would win the case hands down.

Perhaps all would have been different had I remained at Old Trafford, and not had to leave in the summer of 1977 because of my domestic situation. But there was a faction at Old Trafford—and I must specify that I am not referring to the club or its people, for they had always been fantastic to me—who were dedicated to bringing me down.

We used to call them the 'Junior Board' and I'll refer to them again later on. I always felt that they were no good to anybody.

You meet these people 'on the fringe' in football. When things are going well, they're the friends of the players and rubbing shoulders with the important people. But when things aren't so good, they're stirring up the muck.

In my case, they were quite happy to discredit me. With all this ferment in the background, my High Court case was just something else to go wrong. It is a matter of history now that the whole action was a total disaster for me.

The Granada case undoubtedly deprived me of the opportunity of a lot of good jobs. People understandably weren't prepared to take the risk of employing me after all the adverse publicity—certainly not until it had died down.

It cost me, up to the time of the perjury hearing, between

£50,000 and £60,000, which is a lot of money in anybody's book. But that wasn't the saddest thing for me by a long chalk.

What dismayed me most was that the case hurt my family and a lot of people close to me, and a lot of friends into the bargain. I don't suppose it mattered a damn to those who don't like me. Indeed they might even have thought to themselves 'Serve him right' – I don't know.

I could have talked for hours and hours about the Granada case. Now, as far as I'm concerned, it's a blot on my life and it's history now.

But for the historical record – mistake or not – this is my side of the whole Manchester United episode of my life which had its very happy times, but which culminated in sourness and sadness even before the Granada case loomed upon the horizon.

# My Old Trafford Inheritance

MY EXHILARATION at being chosen to guide the destiny of one of the world's greatest clubs was soon to be tempered. For at Old Trafford I inherited a club riddled with cancer–old players, skivers, players who were more concerned with getting rid of the next manager, whoever he may be.

I sussed it out very quickly. I knew I'd been called in to do the dirty work.

Not all the players had a bad attitude, I hasten to add. Just a section. They had virtually taken over. It was like a canker. Because of it, Wilf McGuinness and Frank O'Farrell before me had suffered. And I would have suffered as well if I hadn't gone 'Chop, chop, chop...' and been ruthless and firm.

I'd always felt that to manage Manchester United was my destiny. I had told this to David Meek, the Manchester journalist, some eight or nine years previously.

And the day I was appointed, I walked into the centre of the pitch in the empty ground, looked around me and hummed to myself 'You were meant for me.' And I added the next line of the lyric, too–'I was meant for you,' because that's the way I felt.

It's the only stadium in the world I've ever been in that's absolutely buzzing with atmosphere when it's empty and there isn't a soul inside. It's almost like a cathedral.

To me, a Catholic, it's like going to Rome and walking into St Peter's Square. The whole place is soaked in history and atmosphere.

I was Scotland team manager at the time when the chance came to go to United but there was no way I could turn it down.

The way it happened was like this. I went down to Selhurst Park to see United play Crystal Palace at a time when they were really struggling. United lost 5-0 that day. I knew after that game that the job was mine and that Frank O'Farrell would be sacked the following Tuesday.

In a way, I had strange, mixed feelings about this, for Frank was an old friend of mine, a playing buddy from our Preston days, and was also godfather to one of my boys.

But that's the way it was. And there were three reasons why I gave up the Scotland post to go to Old Trafford, despite the fact that I'd only served one year of a four-year contract.

The first reason was the enormous challenge offered by being the manager of such a famous club. As I say, it had always been my ambition. Secondly, it was for job satisfaction. There wasn't enough work for me in the Scotland post—it didn't keep me busy enough. The third reason was the money.

The salary at that time for being Scotland manager was £7,500 a year—which wasn't a lot—and a car. At the start, I was writing for a local newspaper and I was getting paid as much by them as I was by Scotland, but after only six weeks of doing that, the Scottish FA stepped in and stopped it—and that didn't help.

At Old Trafford, my salary doubled. I'd have gone if it had gone up by only a half.

It's football history now that after the glory days, up to the time I got to Old Trafford, there was a very unsettled period.

Some older players—not all—had undermined Wilf McGuinness and seen him off. Frank had come in, with Malcolm Musgrove, and they had enjoyed a very good playing spell for a few months, until eventually they had started getting at him, too.

So Frank went the same way as Wilf, although he was probably a bit stronger and tried to do something about his problems.

Denis Law said afterwards that Frank O'Farrell came as a stranger, and left as a stranger. That might be true. But the reason could be that like me, he was disappointed with Denis. In fact, Frank later told me this was the case.

And Frank has also told me since that there were lots of times he would have liked to do something about the situation, and tried to, but he was restrained—and not, incidentally by the board. The board never interfered at Old Trafford, and certainly not when I was there.

I think that Frank might have wanted to get rid of certain players but Sir Matt Busby was against it. I also think this was an illustration of something I have always believed—that Matt ran Manchester United with his heart instead of his head.

This brings me to my association with Matt and at the outset I want to make it plain that to this day, I love the man. The only real differences I have ever had with Matt have been since I left the club.

I feel he was partly responsible for my leaving—although naturally my domestic situation helped a considerable amount. But in fairness to him, all the time I was there he was marvellous. When I arrived, I immediately said to him: 'If you ever feel that I'm doing anything wrong, or anything stupid, please let me know about it.'

There might have been the odd minor irritation, an example of which I'll give later. But never once, while I was there, did Matt say 'I think you should play Jones, or I think you should buy Smith.'

Only once, when I bought Jimmy Greenhoff for £100,000 from Stoke City, did he say 'I wouldn't pay any more than that for him, and I wouldn't pay any more than that in wages.'

He wasn't saying to me 'Don't do it.' What he was saying was 'If it was me, that's what I would pay for him, and those are the wages I would pay him.' He was trying to be helpful.

He was always very fair. At board meetings, whenever we discussed the buying of a player, he would go round the table seeking views—and they were a marvellous board of directors—then offer his own opinion.

This was fair enough—he had been a great manager and it was interesting to hear his assessments.

But there was the odd ripple on the waters, from time to time. I recall one instance when we were in Spain on a holiday and the chairman, the late Louis Edwards, gave us a party in his room. Mr Edwards was a lovely man, and believe me he will be sorely missed at that club. The party went on until about four in the morning. Next day Sir Matt asked me about it.

'I believe you had a party in the chairman's room last night,' he said. 'Yes,' I replied. 'The chairman invited all the boys up, asked me if it was okay and I said it was.'

He reminded me about what I had asked him when I first joined the club and that if he felt anything was wrong, he would mention it to me. I said I well remembered it, and he then told me he thought going to the party was wrong, adding 'familiarity breeds contempt'.

I then said to him: 'Now you know how I feel when you play golf with three of my players every Sunday morning.'

I felt he had put me in a position where I had to make that remark. He wasn't very pleased, but he took the point. Overall, I found him a fair man – and certainly for me he was a very powerful ally when he could have been a very powerful enemy.

He and the board had brought me in, but I sometimes wonder how much success he wanted me to have.

People have said to me that although I got the sack from United mainly because of my domestic situation, I was also pushed out because I was becoming too popular at Old Trafford and too well-liked by the chairman. They said that Matt didn't like this, and I'm inclined to believe this.

You see, although I was Matt's and the board's appointment, I feel Matt wouldn't like anyone at Old Trafford to overshadow his record.

And after all, that's only human nature. If I had won three European Cups and three FA Cups while I was in charge, I've no doubt that I wouldn't like it if someone then came in and won four European Cups and four FA Cups.

I always wanted to win everything for the club and Mr Edwards because they took me to Old Trafford. I'd have won the boat race if it had been possible.

I think, looking back and without being blasé, that of the four appointments by Matt and the board, I was the most successful.

And of the four teams under those managers, the team under my charge was the best footballing side they'd had since the good old days. For after me Dave Sexton was a complete disaster.

But I say again, Matt never once interfered with my job, and I couldn't accept the view that was offered by some people that at that time he was a shadow of his former self.

Matt had been a terrific manager with the help of Jimmy Murphy who still does a bit of scouting for the club. Jimmy was a dream of a man and he didn't get as much credit as he was due for the success days at Old Trafford.

In soccer politics, Sir Matt was a big man. Soccer-wise, he's a better politician than Harold Wilson ever was. There was a lot of politics at Old Trafford at the time – the bigger the club the bigger the politics – and as a politician Sir Matt would have tied Sir Harold and Henry Kissinger in knots.

United were great because of Matt down the years, and nobody can take that away from him. I certainly wouldn't want to.

I had my own taste of United politics while I was there, and it wasn't something I sought. It was tied up with a very unsavoury group of people whom we called 'the junior board'.

It was a bit of a joke at the time, but it wasn't always funny.

Who were the junior board? That was the name given to them by the directors, by myself and my first-team coach Tommy Cavanagh. We made a bit of a joke out of it, and I'm sure many United supporters will be tickled to learn about this back-room political side-issue.

I haven't a good word to say for them. The best description I can give of them is that they were hangers-on. They were like bloodsuckers, feeding off the success of the club, and putting down the poison when things weren't going so well.

They were supposed to be Manchester United supporters, and there were only a few of them. They were friends of some of the players, and they liked to think they were friends of the directors, although they were not really.

If the truth were known, they did more harm to the club than good. They used to think they had influence, but they never really had.

In my early months at Old Trafford, I used to get on well with everyone, and go out to dinner with some people there. I found after a while that in doing this, I was getting involved with the politics. I began to think to myself: this isn't going to keep me in the job. So I stopped going out to dinner, and that's when I think some people stopped being for me, and turned against me, just because I wouldn't socialise with them.

From that point on, I had not only to worry about my job, but look over my shoulder at the 'antis', and people like the junior board. But through it all, I always maintained one aim: to do what was best for the club.

Some thought I was doing what was best for Tommy Docherty. But if you do what is good for you and not for the club, you won't last long. You don't count. The club's the biggest thing.

So when I began sorting out the wrongs of the playing side, I wasn't being disrespectful to any players.

I felt that some players who had been great could no longer contribute their best. People like Denis Law, David Sadler, Tony Dunne–and Brian Kidd, who had done a good job, and who parted company with the club with no animosity whatsoever, a great lad.

Tony, too, is a super fellow, a gentleman. I gave him a free transfer–no aggro from him. Tony went on to give Bolton three or four marvellous years' service. Alex Stepney had done a great job for United, although I felt in my last two or three years, when I tried Paddy Roche, that Alex had gone over the hill as well.

Some people thought I was taking this line because these players were Matt's old players. It wasn't that at all. It comes back to what I just said–I was trying to do what was best for the club. The glory days had gone and I had been called in to be the unpopular fellow.

I'd have been a darned sight more unpopular had it not been for a wonderful gesture by Bobby Charlton for which I shall always be grateful.

Bobby had played well for me. Then he came to me one day to tell me he had decided to retire. 'I wanted to tell you first and get your permission to tell Mr Edwards and the board,' he said.

That was superb. He made my job very easy, because there would have come a time when I would have had to say to him 'Bobby, I think it's time for you to hang up your boots.' Now how could that ever have been a popular decision? No way. That's one job I wouldn't have relished.

I think looking back now that I should have appointed Bobby as my No. 2 at United. I'm not saying that things might have been any smoother for me, but in retrospect it would have been a far better decision than my appointment of Pat Crerand–something to which I shall refer later on.

Relegation could easily have resulted in me losing my job a lot earlier. We escaped going down the first season I was there through a lot of hard work and not a little luck, too.

But the following season, 1973-74, we went down. I must say that at that stage I quite expected the sack, but I was reckoning without the intelligence of the board.

Sir Matt and Mr Edwards told me they weren't happy about it. I was even less happy. But would you believe–that weekend they brought me a case of champagne. That was a terrific gesture which helped me to go out and put on a brave face for the Press.

They might well instead have brought a revolver and said: 'Go away and do it quietly.'

We took the Second Division by storm. Gates boomed everywhere, we went straight back up and everyone said we were the best thing that had ever happened to the Second Division. We were–but we'd never wish it again. I disagreed with people who said it was a good thing that we went down.

Everyone knows now that we reached Wembley two years running. We lost the first Final to Southampton but even though I was choked to bits I phoned Lawrie McMenemy at his banquet, wished him well, and told him it would be our turn the following year.

And it was. But when I look back on it, it was crazy to lose to Southampton and then beat Liverpool.

All the time the cards were stacking up against me and my domestic situation was very much in turmoil at this stage of my career. I knew a lot of people were trying to get me out, particularly the junior board. Even players who had left, felt they shouldn't have left and were stirring it up. Why?

Because when you're a manager, and you get rid of a player, naturally he's resentful. It's human nature. He doesn't realise it's best for the club – that's of no interest to him. All he thinks is 'That so-and-so got rid of me.'

He's played for the best club in the world. And when anybody leaves Manchester United as a player, there's only one way he goes, and that's down. So instead of taking the view that he'd played for United, wasn't quite good enough, and is still in football, he takes the narrow view. Being resentful, if he can't get back at you on the football pitch, he'll try to do it in other ways.

My domestic situation was a heaven-sent opportunity for the people who were trying to get me out. I did something for them that they'd never have been able to do themselves. When they saw the news in the paper of my sacking, they must have held all-night parties in Manchester.

They talk about the hooligans in soccer, but this sort of person is even worse, in my book.

# 3
# A Law Unto Himself

WHEN I CAME to Manchester United in December 1972, it seemed to me that Denis Law was at a stage of his career when he wasn't worried about how he played. All he was concerned with was how long he would go on playing.

Looking at his injury file, on my arrival at Old Trafford, I had my suspicions about his attitude. It looked to me that under Wilf McGuinness and Frank O'Farrell, he might not have been producing 100 per cent. Under myself he certainly did not. It seemed to me he had been saving himself for some time–and I felt very sad.

I had played in Denis's first international against Wales in 1958. He was even then a marvellous, world-class player, and we were very good friends. Through the years he became a celebrated player of enormous ability. But when I went to Old Trafford, I just couldn't believe it. When I had been the Scotland team manager, I had chosen him for his country. He had done a good job in the past, and he did a good job for me, too.

Now, he had stopped trying. A typical example of the way I found things with him at United was this: he would be injured on the Saturday after the game. He would sometimes come in for treatment on the Sunday, sometimes not. He'd be in for treatment Monday, Tuesday, Wednesday and Thursday, a loosener up on the Friday, and be ready for Saturday. I smelled it a mile away.

Supporters don't see these things. They have their heroes–and quite rightly so. Bobby Charlton, for example. What a marvellous professional, what a credit to the game.

He was in a different class. But you would get people like Law, and to a degree Pat Crerand, who hadn't a good word to say about

Bobby Charlton. They didn't think he could play. They'd ask me how I thought he'd performed and I'd tell them. Even on the occasions when Bobby hadn't had a great game, he'd given 100 per cent. But whatever happened, it seemed to be a fixation with them – 'how's Bobby doing?'

One point at which I got into trouble in the High Court about the Denis Law business was when I was asked by the defence counsel whether it was a manager's job to familiarise himself with all the players' contracts and I replied that it was. 'Did you do this?' he asked and I replied 'yes, I did.'

Then he left it for a day or so and when he went back to it again, he asked me what sort of wages Law had been on. I said I didn't know exactly.

'But you said you read the contracts,' he said. I replied that I meant I had sifted through them. He then asked me: 'Did you read them, or didn't you?' I answered: 'Not all of them.'

'Yet before, you said you did – and now today you're saying you didn't. You're telling lies.'

I didn't say I was telling lies – but I couldn't deny the implication. I also had to agree under cross-examination that evidence I gave about the release of the news of Law's free transfer to the Press turned out to be untrue.

Now one of the chief points of contention between Denis Law and myself has been Law's claim that I had promised him a job for life at Old Trafford, and in any event, that he would be youth team coach. But at the particular time that he was talking about, Denis Law wouldn't have crossed the road to watch a game of soccer. Even when Denis was substitute for the first team, he wouldn't sit on the bench – he admitted that himself. He would sit in the dressing room. I'd want a coach to be more committed than that.

Incidentally, Law wasn't a qualified coach. I accept that this doesn't necessarily matter. Bob Paisley and Cloughie, I believe, aren't qualified coaches, but you'd be hard put to find two more successful managers in the game today.

But the main point was: how could I possibly offer Denis Law a job for life at Old Trafford when I had only a three-year contract myself? The assertion was completely untrue. In any case, we had a good staff at the time. I couldn't have promised anyone any job.

Denis had a year of his contract to run, and I suggested to him that as I was building for the future, I would be prepared to give him a free transfer.

Now a lot of players are delighted to get a free. I've had players come to me and ask for a free so that they can get some money from their next club, under the counter, tax-free.

Denis wasn't pleased – but he certainly wasn't surprised. When I recommended it to the board, Sir Matt Busby was against it. He thought Denis could do us a job for another year or so. But the club gave Denis £5,000 tax-free for the remainder of his contract for that year, and he got the free. He could have stayed if he had wished – his contract wasn't finished. He didn't have to go.

Denis felt getting a free would affect his testimonial match. But I don't think it did – on the contrary, it helped it. I think it was appreciated that all I was doing was what was best for Manchester United.

Later, there was more fuel on the fire through the crazy situation in which the Press said Denis – then playing for Manchester City – scored the goal that relegated us. That was rubbish – United were doomed to go down. If we'd scored 20 goals it wouldn't have saved us then.

It is difficult to remember exactly what happened seven years ago, as I discovered when giving evidence in the High Court.

It was put to me that whatever I said to Denis one week, I changed my mind the next – but I say I didn't. It stands to reason. Why should I go to the board one week with a recommendation for a free transfer and then a week later, after, with the exception of Sir Matt, they had rubber-stamped it, go back and say 'I've changed my mind – I think we'll keep him.'

The first thing the board would say, and justifiably, would be 'What sort of manager have we got? He can't even make up his mind.'

The other big bone of contention was over Denis's anger that I released the announcement of his free transfer to the Press without telling him that I was going to.

Now in all honesty, I admit that I probably did mention it

at least to David Meek, the *Manchester Evening News* man who covers United. But the news could well have got out in other ways.

At that time Denis was a great pal of Crerand, Alex Stepney and Willie Morgan. They and their wives, and Paddy McGrath, who was a friend of Sir Matt's and a local hero with the players (I used to call him 'Mr. X') would have dinner together on a Saturday night.

Obviously Denis would have said to them 'I've got a free' and my reckoning is that it could have filtered out to the Press by this route.

There was another way it could have got out. Denis was very friendly with Matt, who, of course, attended board meeting discussions. He also played golf with people like Law, Stepney, Crerand and Morgan. And I think that human nature being what it is, Matt would naturally say something about it to them.

As far as the court case is concerned, everyone knows I lost the case and I also lost a lot of money. But it's been a great lesson to me, and to any friends of mine who might have this sort of court case coming up, I'd say forget it.

The only people who win in court are solicitors. They lie in the south of France drinking champagne.

I made a mistake. I've paid very dearly for it and so have a lot of friends. It's been a humiliating experience for me and them. But I'm a type of person who doesn't hate anybody.

I dislike Denis Law, but I've no axe to grind with Willie Morgan, no matter what people say. Willie was a good player for me and a good professional and the only thing I was guilty of over him was leaving him out of the first-team at Manchester United because unfortunately, through the eye injury, he wasn't playing as well as previously. If he wants to think I sang silly little songs about him then he can, but I can tell him that I've got more to do with my time than things like that.

# 4
# The Headline That Never Was

ONE MAN I fell out with during my time at Old Trafford–irreparably, as it turned out–was Pat Crerand.

During this period there occurred an incident that could so easily have resulted in sensational newspaper headlines.

Pat loved Manchester United and had been a very good player for them. That's a fact and no one can deny it. But I made a mistake over Pat and I went to the board and admitted it.

I appointed him my No. 2 and in retrospect, if the biggest mistake of my life was in bringing the court case against Willie Morgan and Granada, then appointing Pat as my assistant was the next biggest.

I must declare an interest at the outset: I dislike Pat Crerand. His envy of greater talents (like Bobby Charlton's) was always clear to me. In my opinion his soccer experiences have made him a bitter person.

My reasons for appointing him No. 2 were twofold: I did it because in all fairness, at the time, I thought he could do a good job for the club, and also because I thought it was what Sir Matt wanted.

And I am sure that it is because of this, and because of something involving Glasgow Celtic which I shall explain later, that he has developed a vindictive attitude towards me.

He was my assistant for a few months when I realised I had made a misjudgment over it and I decided to tell the board this.

The great thing about soccer management is that you have to make decisions. But if you make a bad one, then I say: admit it. If you buy a player and he turns out a bad investment, why then try to prove he's a good player? Admit your mistake and cut your losses.

Between us, Sir Matt and I got Pat a testimonial at Old Trafford after seven years' service. He received £46,000 and good luck to him – he was a good player and he deserved it. But I felt there was no alternative but to inform the board I had made a mistake.

Where I went wrong with Pat and my assessment of him, was over his lack of organisation. He's the most disorganised man you could ever meet.

He was in charge of the youth team as assistant manager, and they would go on tour. I remember one occasion when the youth team left the ground at 7.30 in the morning to go to the airport and Pat turned up at 8.30. He was half-dressed and looking to cash a cheque. All that should have been done days before, and would have been by an organised person. He was in charge of young players. What example was that to them?

The important thing to stress about Pat and his departure from United was that I didn't sack him.

At the time of his testimonial, he told me and the board that he had decided – and I am sure he spoke to Sir Matt about it – that he wanted to try his luck with coaching.

My opinion of his coaching is that it hardly runs beyond five-a-sides. He talks a good game of soccer and that's the finish.

The board were great to him. They paid him a year's wages – he was on about £10,000 or £11,000 a year at the time – and I think they gave him his car, and they wished him well. But it was his decision to leave the club. The board didn't say to him 'You're no longer assistant manager,' and neither did I. I knew it would get back to him that I'd said I'd made a mistake in appointing him. So he decided to go his own way.

Then came the extraordinary incident after the 1976 FA Cup Final when we lost to Southampton. Back in Manchester there was a civic reception at the Town Hall and Pat – who by this time had left the club – was there as a guest of Sir Matt's.

I was as sick as a parrot, as they say, after losing the Final. Any manager would be, of course. But I was delighted for big Lawrie

McMenemy, for Ted Bates, and for their chairman George Reader—lovely people.

I went to the toilet after the coffee break, and Pat Crerand came in, threatening me. There were a couple of young players in there at the time, and I could see that he intended getting me involved in something distasteful. I thought he was looking for a fight.

Fortunately for me, Tommy Cavanagh came walking in just then. I think someone had told him that Pat had gone to the toilet and knowing him and what he was like, Tommy went to him and said 'Come on, Pat, behave yourself,' or something like that.

Pat had just wanted me to raise my voice and that would have been another incident. The headlines would have read 'Docherty and Crerand in Fight in Toilet!' That would have been nice, wouldn't it?

I came right out and said to Sir Matt: 'I just went in there for a wash and that idiot came in, and what he said to me . . . You've got to do something about him, because he's a head case.' Matt looked at me and tutted, saying, 'That's all we need.'

Matt's a lovely man—he doesn't want that sort of aggravation. Pat should have known better anyway because he was Matt's guest at the dinner.

The other thing that bugged Pat was that he thought, quite wrongly as it happened, that I had deprived him of a job with my old club Celtic.

Jock Stein was Celtic manager at the time but, coming back from holiday, had a car crash. They were looking around for an assistant to Jock. One day the telephone in my office rang. On the other end of the line was an old friend, Jim Farrell, a Celtic director.

He explained that they were looking for a No. 2 because Jock was incapacitated and asked me: 'What about Pat Crerand?'

I replied: 'Socially, as a fellow to go out with, great company. But I must be honest with you. I don't think he'd do you any good as assistant manager.'

He asked me my honest opinion and I gave it. Now if I'd said 'He'll do you a marvellous job,' that would have been quite wrong. If it hadn't come off, and I'm sure it wouldn't have, it would have reflected on my judgment, and Mr Farrell could have come back to me and said 'You're a fine fellow, Tommy Docherty – recommending Pat Crerand.'

When Pat tackled me about it and said I had stopped him getting the job at Celtic, I said 'You're crazy.' I told him I'd been asked by Farrell if I thought he would have been a good assistant for Jock Stein, and I'd said I didn't think so. 'So you deprived me of the job,' Crerand said.

'No I didn't – I gave my honest opinion,' I told him. 'I'd have been delighted, as it was my old club as well, to say that you would have been a great man for the job, but I couldn't, just as you might not think I'm the right man for Manchester United. That's your opinion.' I went on: 'Don't you think, Pat, that if Jock Stein had really wanted you as his assistant, he'd have appointed you himself, or at least asked Mr Farrell to get you to come up and see him. He didn't need to have asked Tommy Docherty's opinion of you. He'd have sorted it out without speaking to Mr Farrell.'

Pat couldn't see this and thought what I said had deprived him of the job, which wasn't correct.

So I am sure those are the two reasons why Pat's antagonistic towards me. In addition, he must have been disappointed to have left United at his own request, only to see us reach two successive Cup Finals, and win the second one.

He could see me then becoming very strong at Manchester United and eventually, though I had no wish to do so, becoming as strong and as popular as Sir Matt.

Now Matt was in a different class, a super man. And it puzzled me why he hung around with such people who couldn't do him any good.

Pat went on to Northampton Town as manager. Since then he's not been in football.

There was some more mud flying round from Pat in my direction over another matter, which did in fact make the headlines. That was about George Best – and thereby hangs another tale...

# 5
# The Best and Worst
# of George

As a player, George Best was one of the very few whom you could justifiably describe as a genius. He was world-class, and a smashing young fellow. But from the time he arrived at Manchester United, he was very badly handled.

Before my spell at Old Trafford, he had given his best years to the club. But oh, what might have been...

When he became a star, he met and mixed with the wrong people—people who like to be seen with the stars, and who hung on to him like leeches. At the club he was subject to no real discipline, and by that I mean sensible discipline. He did what he wanted, and got away with murder.

It has been said that he was a victim of his own situation—that of being a super-star and someone who was made a folk-hero by the youngsters, especially the girls.

But everything that happened to him, good or bad, was engineered by himself. People close to him knew they had a super-star on their hands, but he drove them mad. And I'm thinking particularly of his agent Ken Stanley, a nice guy. Ken would make appointments for George to go here and there, but he wouldn't turn up. He let sponsors and commercial people down time after time.

What went wrong with George? It's a question I've often been asked. My own personal view is that if George, who is now happily married with a little boy, which is super, had got married much earlier, the stability and responsibility that marriage brings would have made a vast difference to him.

Now I appreciate that you just can't say, to order: 'You're a super-star, you're 18—I'm going to get you a woman and you're going to marry and have two or three kids, and if you don't you're going to be finished.' But something like that might have changed it all for him . . .

Ken Stanley was a good agent. But maybe, George should also have got himself a personal manager to look after him, to make sure he toed the line and deal with all the fierce attention the Press gave him. He should also have had a staff handling his mountain of mail and taking a lot of the pressure off his shoulders, allowing him to do what he was marvellous at—playing football.

There was an instance when Sir Matt felt things were getting out of hand with George and sent him to live with Pat Crerand. Now how was Pat going to look after Besty?

I had George with me for several months at Old Trafford and found him a smashing lad—it was an awful shame that things deteriorated for him, and for the whole United team in the late 1960s.

I felt the same thing applied to the rest of the side as applied to him. If they had received a little more discipline, and by that I don't mean the rigid sergeant-major type, they would have won a lot more trophies.

They were a great side, but if they had been a bit better organised tactically, they could have won the European Cup half a dozen times.

Curiously enough, I felt they actually won the European Cup in 1968 with the poorest United side over that period. The players were doing what they wanted, when with more discipline and dedication, they'd have been more successful.

I know people have always said that Sir Matt let them go out and play the way they wanted, and because of that they got results. I maintain the results would have been better had there been a measure of discipline. When the team started to fall away, that was because most of the star players—George included—weren't working hard enough. They felt they always had their wonderful skill to fall back upon.

They had the skill all right. But skill without working is not enough, because soccer's about running as well as about skill. If you've got skill and you're prepared to work hard, no one will beat you.

What a shame it all was. Just think of what they had. Bobby Charlton, what a credit to soccer. Best, a genius. Denis Law was a great player, and Crerand very good. Nobby Stiles, David Herd, good players. Bill Foulkes, a good, dedicated pro.

I'll give you a good example of why things went wrong for George, and for United, and why the lack of discipline finally became the team's undoing.

George himself admitted in a newspaper not very long ago that in 1970 Wilf McGuinness, who was then the manager, caught him in bed with a woman an hour and a half before the League Cup semi-final with Aston Villa at Villa Park.

Best should have been sent straight home, and I know for a fact that was what Wilf wanted to do—he told me so. But Sir Matt said no, they couldn't do without him. And they still lost the match. So what chance had Wilf got after that?

This was another instance of the players at that time doing what they wanted—you could call it player-power. That's also why the players loved Sir Matt so much—because he let them do what they liked.

I love Matt. He loves his game and he loves people to enjoy it. I am sure he could have been hard—but being hard is one thing, and doing something about it is another. It may be that he felt that by letting his players have free expression, he would get the best out of them. But I am certain if he had been firmer, his record today would have been even more terrific than it is.

So in this environment, George Best went downhill and it got to the stage when things just became ludicrous with all sorts of teams coming in and asking if they could hire George out for one or two games.

Round about this time, George was doing his Howard Hughes bit—coming and going and disappearing. It was easier to find Martin Bormann than it was to find George. Somehow Pat Crerand could always trace him, and so could the 'junior board'.

All sorts of stupid offers were coming in for George to make appearances for people – from the boys' brigade to the boy scouts. Sir Matt Busby summed it up perfectly when he said 'Why don't we give the boy a free transfer, because it's becoming a bit of a flea-circus. Everybody wants to hire him ... it's a joke.' But the board were trying to do their best by George. If he'd put his mind to it, he'd have been worth a lot of money to the club.

At this time, there was the business of George going to play for non-League Dunstable – and it was over this that Pat Crerand made an allegation against me in a newspaper article that was totally untrue.

I got a phone call one day from Barry Fry, the Dunstable manager, asking if George could play for Dunstable for a couple of games. The club had set down a fee for this sort of appearance – I think it was £1,000 a game, or something like that. So I told Barry to get in touch with the United secretary Les Olive, and with Best himself, and it could be arranged.

Pat claimed that I received £2,000 for letting Best play for Dunstable, but in actual fact, clubs wanting George to play didn't have to approach me as the manager – they were able to get him by paying the club the fee they wanted, and sorting out George's own fee with him. Any club wanting him at that time could have got him by dealing with the club, not with individuals like me.

The secretary had to deal with the forms, and George had to sign something himself, and that was that. To say I received money was untrue.

# 6
# A Great Chairman
# –and a Pal

VIVID THOUGH my memory is of people who were less than friendly towards me at Old Trafford–and even downright antagonistic–the recollection of one friendship I made there will always be uppermost in my mind.

Louis Edwards was my chairman during the five and a half years I was there and in my book, he was a great, great man–and I make no apologies for repeating the word.

He was more than a chairman, he was a pal. Today, I miss Louis Edwards so much. As a result of his death, Manchester United are the poorer.

Even now, whenever I go into a hotel with a football team, I half expect to see Louis Edwards sitting in the bar, smiling, and saying 'Have a glass of champagne, Tom.'

The only regret I have concerning Mr Edwards arose from an incident after I left the club. He was reported in a newspaper–and was misquoted–as saying that 'we've got a new manager in Dave Sexton–and we've got a gentleman' and I thought the remark implied that I wasn't a gentleman.

I can be a gentleman sometimes, other times I cannot. I was very annoyed at the time. I took exception to it, and I served Mr Edwards with a writ.

It was a stupid and a wrong thing to do–I know that now. It was wrong because he never did me a bad turn in his life.

He was in a different class to most of the other chairmen I had worked with, and knew, in football. If he had one fault, it was that he was too generous. That apart, he was marvellous all the time I was in charge, and in my view down the years he did a lot more for Manchester United than he ever got credit for.

This is one of the reasons why his death not only filled me with tremendous sorrow but also made me angry. He was like a father to me – he never refused me anything. Practically every time I saw him, he'd say 'Who are you going to buy – do you want some money?' He was unbelievable.

I could never say a wrong word about Louis Edwards – and that goes for the Manchester United board of directors as well. So you can imagine my reaction, because of my feelings for him, and also in the aftermath of the Morgan–Granada court case, when Granada TV sent someone to see me one day.

He came to my house, and told me he was preparing some material for the programme 'World In Action.'

'We're doing a programme about Manchester United,' he said.

My response was terse to say the least. 'If your programme was dying of cancer, and I had the cure, I wouldn't supply it,' I said. He must have known I might take sort that of stance, particularly because of my own experiences with the Company which were still all too fresh in my mind.

He pressed on doggedly. 'We're going into the share issue at Manchester United and Mr Frank O'Farrell has already spoken to us. We're wondering if you would contribute to it, or comment on it.'

By this time I was beginning to boil. 'I've told you already,' I said, 'you are not one of my favourite programmes. Secondly, the share issue at Manchester United never had, and still doesn't have, anything to do with me. Mr Edwards, Matt Busby, and all the board at Manchester United, as far as I am concerned, are friends of mine. My days there were nothing but happy.

'All I was concerned with at United was that I was in charge of the playing side. So thirdly – piss off.'

And away he went.

Quite some time later, I was sitting watching television when the programme 'World In Action' came up on the screen.

They stated they were going into the business of the issue of the shares at Manchester United. I was absolutely appalled.

As I saw it, they were implying that Mr Edwards was doing—or attempting to do—something that was illegal, something that wasn't quite right.

A little while later, Louis Edwards was dead. It all made me very bitter.

If you knew Louis Edwards like I did, he was a lovely big, warm and hospitable man. He couldn't do you a bad turn if he tried. I'm not really bothered about, or interested in, the shares.

All I know is that Mr Edwards, who had heart trouble anyway, had been put on the rack. And he was a tremendous worrier.

If he was having his dinner, and the soup was a bit late, he'd worry about it. That's the way he was. And as I listened to the programme with mounting horror, I could visualise what must have been going through his mind when he first heard about this programme and the enquiries that people were making.

When he thought about all those dreadful people who would be phoning him about it, he would worry himself to death. On top of that, the mere thought of a possible case coming up against him would have been just too much for him.

I think maybe he died because of the thought of going into the witness-box—he couldn't have handled it. He wasn't the type of person to have withstood all that sort of pressure. And in addition, the realisation that his beloved club might have a big question-mark against its integrity would have weighed heavily on his mind.

The confrontation on my doorstep with the Granada people wasn't the only time I was invited to put the boot in on Manchester United after I left.

There was the occasion when I was at Queen's Park Rangers for my second spell in 1979-80. One day a representative of one of the big national newspapers offered to set me up for life financially if I would say something derogatory about Louis Edwards and Matt Busby.

They were talking in terms of over £100,000 in return for me stirring up some muck. They thought that because of the manner in which I lost my job at United, and the domestic situation with Mary which caused it, that I would want to get back at them.

But I didn't—and never have done. All I want for Manchester United is to see them successful, especially after my wonderful five and a half years with them. So I showed them the door as well.

Ken Shellito, my No. 2 at Preston who was with me at the time, was a witness to this approach.

That man from the newspaper had me figured wrong. He didn't reckon on my love for United—my affection for the club. I worked there with the best support in the world, a great staff. Everything about the club was class, charisma.

Louis Edwards and his board were always good to me and tried to make my path as a manager as easy as possible, particularly where money for players was concerned. The chairman even supported me at the time when I was trying to lure Peter Shilton to Old Trafford, though the story of this 'transfer that never was' was given one or two different versions at the time, and later.

What happened was this. I would have liked Shilton and the board were prepared to put up the money. But Peter, at that time, was on £400 a week at Stoke City, and Sir Matt and another director were against us paying him a wage like that, at that time.

They felt they couldn't commit themselves to such a salary. My idea was to transfer either Alex Stepney or Paddy Roche plus money for Shilton. But because there was a disagreement over the wage we were prepared to offer, the deal fell through.

That was one of the rare occasions when I went to the board and didn't get what I wanted. Looking back, how many managers can boast of a relationship like that with their employers?

Of course, the situation which came to a head over my private life in the spring of 1977 placed the chairman in a very difficult position.

It meant the parting of the ways and I left behind me a man of whom I shall always be very fond and who provided me with one of those friendships in football which can be so rewarding, and later on, provided me with memories which are only pleasant.

At this stage, not only my soccer career hit the headlines again. This time my private life was under the dazzling glare of the mass publicity that the media are so good at providing.

And it meant also that Mary Brown had to face it as well...

# 7
# The Mary Brown Affair

WELL OVER a thousand managers have lost their jobs with Football League clubs since the war, and for a variety of reasons. But I reckon I must be the first one to get the chop because of falling in love with another man's wife!

Because that's the only thing I was guilty of in what the newspapers have called 'The Mary Brown Affair'.

Mary was the wife of Laurie Brown, who had been Manchester United's physiotherapist during my time at Old Trafford. Laurie remained there after I left until just before the 1981-82 season when, ironically, he too got the sack when the new manager Ron Atkinson brought in his own staff to work with him.

I maintain that I would have been at Old Trafford to this day but for the Mary Brown business—but at the same time I would stress that I don't regret what I did for one moment. Mary and I have been together since, and we now have a lovely little girl, Grace.

What a load of moralising went on at that time, especially from some of the media writers with the 'holier-than-thou' angles in their articles. Some of those doing the writing, to my knowledge, had plenty of skeletons in their private cupboards!

When it all came out, I quickly discovered that two or three people at Old Trafford whom I'd thought were my friends—and I don't mean directors—weren't really friends at all.

This is my version of the Mary Brown affair, and you may think it is a somewhat different account than some of the sensationally written pieces in the papers.

Of course, it was difficult for the club—I fully acknowledge that, and I must confess that I wouldn't have liked to have been in the position of Louis Edwards and his board, particularly with the Catholic influence which exists at Old Trafford.

I felt it was a personal moral issue, and that I should have carried on as manager. All the supporters of a club want is for their team to be successful and to be playing good, attractive soccer. At the time, that was what they were getting. We'd just won the FA Cup and we were back on the right road.

If I'd been working in the same circumstances for British Leyland they'd have probably given me a new 10-year contract!

I first met Mary about six or seven months after I joined the club—that was around the middle of 1973. But it wasn't for a couple of years that we began to form an attachment for each other. We would go out for a meal and a chat—nothing else. We just enjoyed each other's company.

It developed from that point to a time when our feelings for each other became very strong. And over this period, the situation with my own marriage had become difficult anyway.

I got stroppy with my wife, and she got stroppy with me—she knew something wasn't right. And I was so wrapped up in my job that the whole thing became very difficult for both of us. In fact it was getting impossible.

As for the Press line that I 'ran away with the physiotherapist's wife' that's absolute rubbish, at least in the literal sense. I never ran anywhere—the only running I did may have been up and down stairs in the house all three of us shared for over a year!

That was Mary's mother's house. Yes, we actually lived in the same building for all that time.

It is impossible for me to believe Laurie was unaware that Mary and I were living together at the time, for he was occupying a part of the house upstairs. Mary would go upstairs to put her kids to bed at night and then come back downstairs to spend the night with me.

I was frightened to death. I thought all he had to say to Matt was 'Look, he's going out with my wife, what are you going to do about it?' and Matt would have probably cut the legs off me.

Mary and I wanted to be with each other more than anything

and at this stage I had the chance of signing a new four-year contract with the club.

I could have signed, but I didn't. I thought it over, and because they were such nice people, decided that I'd tell them about Mary and me. I wanted to be fair to them.

I know that was the right thing to do. People have said since that the club must have known about it for some time, but that couldn't be.

Martin Edwards, who is now the club's chairman, was the first person I told – and he knew nothing up to that point. Martin's first words to me were: 'Tom, it's one of those things. It's been happening since Adam and Eve. It's a private matter and nothing to do with the football club at all.'

That was about three weeks before the fateful meeting of the board in Louis Edwards's house when the decision was taken that I must leave Old Trafford. Les Olive, the club secretary, and Sir Matt were both on holiday at the time of my conversation with Martin Edwards and they read about it in the newspapers.

My wife knew what was happening because I told her, and she virtually told me 'On your way' which from her point of view was about the only thing she could say.

Mary and I told Laurie, and the club got me to take the youth team for a short tour of Portugal, the idea being that this would allow things to 'cool off' a bit.

It was a nice break, but I was away from Mary for a week, and I was wondering how she was coping, particularly with all the publicity back in England, and her house being besieged by reporters.

By this time, I felt the whole world must have known about us. So back I came to England to face the Press again.

Even then, the official club attitude expressed in comments by both Louis and Martin Edwards, was that it was a private matter and there was no need for me to leave Manchester United.

But it was then that the 'unseen forces' began to get to work and suddenly everything changed. First of all, on the morning of the vital board meeting at Louis Edwards's home, Laurie Brown, and a friend of his who used to work at United, went to see the Edwardses.

Eventually I was summoned to the meeting and was asked to resign. I declined, saying I had done nothing to be ashamed of.

By this time, Sir Matt had returned from holiday and had said to me 'You bloody fool . . . why didn't you let me know about all this?' I replied: 'Matt, you were away out of the country. And it wouldn't have made any difference. But it's nice of you to show concern.'

The other 'behind the scenes' aspect to be considered would have been the Catholic influence, not so much at the club, but in the city. I would expect the Catholic fraternity to have prodded Matt and said 'We can't have this sort of thing going on,' and suchlike.

I have been told since—and I must say I've no means of knowing whether this is true or not—that one or two of the directors' wives had suggested 'If Tommy doesn't go, we'll not come back to the club again.'

My attitude all along has been that a man should be judged on his ability at his job, and not on his private life. What sickened me was the big moral stance taken by some of the Press writers. If falling in love with another woman is bad behaviour, then many others are also guilty.

I've had a close-at-hand view of the way some of the members of the media have behaved on tours abroad. Who are they to write about morals? I've often wondered whether they had a prick of conscience when they were writing their stories, questioning whether Manchester United could put up with this sort of thing.

I didn't make things easy for Louis Edwards. But I certainly made it easy for the people in the club who wanted to sack me, to do just that. Matt would have been under a lot of pressure locally to get rid of me.

But what about other people connected with football and their domestic problems? Chairmen, directors, managers, players, press, television presenters—I can give you an example of each with marital problems. So what? It hasn't affected their jobs.

I would have left home anyway, even without the Mary Brown

affair. After our Cup Final victory over Liverpool in 1977, I'd had enough. I was being dreadful to my wife, and my family was suffering. I must have been an awful person to live with just then.

At the Cup Final, I ignored my wife completely – looking back, that was a terrible thing to do. But other people should have a conscience in all this, too; wasn't it harsh on me to lose my job because I fell in love with another woman?

The only regret I have over all this was that it hurt people. Laurie Brown was hurt, and so was my family.

But that's life and these things happen. It was a sad ending to my association with a great club for which I shall always have a special place in my heart.

And looking at Old Trafford now from the outside, it hurts me to see what happened to my team after I'd gone.

# 8
# The Right and Wrong Decisions

MANCHESTER UNITED made a mistake when they sacked me in 1977 over something that had nothing whatsoever to do with football. Perhaps they made an even bigger mistake when they appointed Dave Sexton to succeed me. And in my reckoning, they boobed again after they got rid of him.

For when big Lawrie McMenemy turned down the chance to go to Old Trafford because he thought he'd be better off staying with Southampton, I'd have turned to Bobby Charlton.

This is in no way to detract from the abilities of Ron Atkinson, the man now facing the task of making United great again.

He was not first choice, but he won't worry about that—and he may well turn out to be the best in the long run. That remains to be seen.

Why Bobby? Several reasons. He's a great fellow, knows the game inside out, and the managerial experience he gained at Preston North End would have stood him in good stead.

I don't even know if they'd considered him, or even if he would have accepted, but I think he would have.

As a PRO man, bingo! Licence to print money. He's loved everywhere, he did a marvellous job for England, and everywhere he goes, everyone knows Bobby Charlton.

It would have been tailor-made for them—the return of the favourite son. When I look at Bobby in terms of a United manager, I would have to look for something wrong—but I can't find anything. The sponsors they would have had with a fellow like that in charge would have been untrue. He was right there, sitting on their doorstep.

My successor Dave Sexton was appointed because he was a nice man—it was a sort of backlash over what had happened over me and Mary. Dave is as straight as a dye, the quiet type. They got what they appointed and they deserved what they got.

Dave was well-liked at Chelsea by the players, and at Queen's Park Rangers, and at United. He was well liked because he's soft. Some players don't like a firm man—they like a manager or a coach whom they can twist round their little fingers.

Not all players are like this, thank goodness. The sensible ones are fully aware that guidance, organisation and sensible discipline are absolutely essential from a manager running the club. These players have respect for a firm man.

Ron Saunders is a firm man, so is Bob Paisley, and Cloughie. And so am I. You wouldn't try to pull the wool over their eyes. But you might with Dave.

Now he's gone to Coventry City, he's taken over a relatively unsuccessful side—the first time this has happened to him since he left Orient. When he took over from me at Chelsea, from Gordon Jago at QPR and from me at United, he took over three damned good sides.

He tripped up at Chelsea because he couldn't handle your Osgoods and your Hudsons; he went to QPR and after a good spell when they finished second in the First Division they started falling apart; and at United, he inherited a great, young side, and failed to consolidate.

And what's more, the style of football his team played drove away the supporters from Old Trafford.

United shouldn't have appointed him in the first instance because he isn't their type of person. But having done that, they should have sacked him a couple of years earlier instead of waiting until 1981. United took a lot of stick from certain sections of the media for sacking Dave, but they did the right thing.

Martin Edwards made a rod for his own back, through his inexperience as a chairman after succeeding his father, by not acting sooner. The criticism he took because United won their last seven games of the season, was a lot of rot.

Maybe Martin Edwards was sticking to the formula, agreed by the League clubs in recent times, not to sack a manager during the season.

He deserves a pat on the back for what he did eventually, for he wasn't letting those last seven victories in a row disguise the fact that the type of football United were playing was not entirely pleasing the fans.

A lot of chairmen would have taken the view that those seven wins meant things would be better the following season. But Martin Edwards couldn't see it getting any better, and I think he was dead right. So although United's final position in the table wasn't all that bad, the image had deteriorated, the fans were worried and the club were taking in less money.

Success can be gauged in lots of ways—winning cups and winning leagues. But success is also about balancing the books.

A manager can only play football according to the type of players at his disposal. Now Ron Atkinson won a reputation at West Bromwich Albion for encouraging attacking football. Now he has had to pick up the threads at United. I wish him well.

It's one of the accepted facts of football that when a new manager comes in that the players are all for him—complimentary to him.

It made me smile a little while after Dave took over from me when I read some comments by Sammy McIlroy to the effect that 'We're a better team now than the team Doc had,' and Jimmy Nicholl said they were more organised.

As I look back on my life, and I think about United and the four years they had under Dave Sexton, I ask myself 'What did they win?'

If they were such a good team as Sammy and Jimmy made out, and were better organised and better disciplined, what have they won to show for it?

All right: under me, the club were relegated, but at least we bounced back and got to Wembley two years running, and not many clubs do that.

I accepted total responsibility for United going down into the

Second Division. It was my fault. They would have been perfectly within their rights to sack me at that point. In fact, I felt so bad about letting a great club like that fall into the Second Division, I felt I deserved to be shot.

Matt and Louis Edwards, however, told me: 'We don't want you worrying. We know we're on the right lines. We'll be great again.' They were terrific about it. And we were on the right lines. We went through the Second Division like a knife through butter.

I have strong views about the amount of money in current football. There's too much nowadays and players' demands are killing the game.

I managed to buy some fine players. Martin Buchan was probably the best. Stuart Pearson came from Hull, and Stewart Houston I also bought – both good pros.

I also bought Lou Macari – another good pro, but I always had the feeling with him that he needed an incentive to give of his best. He was an incredible player when he put his mind to it, but his mind sometimes needed to be concentrated.

The Greenhoff brothers I also put in the category of good professionals. Because of their attitude, and that of most of the team I built up, we were able to reach those two FA Cup finals.

After the one in 1976 against Southampton, I was sick. I was so sure we would win – and that wasn't being big-headed – that when we beat Liverpool the following year, it was almost an anticlimax.

We had been such hot favourites against the Saints, and after that, I thought we'd no chance of beating Liverpool.

It was smashing to be at Wembley two years on the trot, but today I can't remember an awful lot about the Liverpool game, for there was such a lot on my mind at the time what with the business over Mary and so on.

I always say that nice people don't win anything – they only come second. But the nice people won when Southampton took the Cup. It was great to see them achieving something, even though it was at our expense.

Curiously enough, we were paired with them in the following season in the fifth round, when we beat them 2-1 after a 2-2 draw at The Dell.

Before the match with Villa in the sixth round, Lawrie McMenemy sent me a telegram saying – 'All the best, wee man – I hope it's your turn this year.'

It was our turn and we were especially pleased because that year Liverpool were all set to win everything. They took the First Division title, and a few days after we beat them at Wembley, they won the European Cup beating Borussia Moenchengladbach in Rome.

Looking back, I'm glad that in the playing and results sense, my last few days at Old Trafford ended on a high note.

But I was making headlines again ... and you will have gathered that some of the Press weren't my favourite people. Not for the first time, I reckoned I was getting a raw deal from the media men.

# 9
# The Media Connection

DURING THE whole time I have been a coach or a manager—and that adds up now to 20 years—I have had a curious love-hate relationship with the Press.

I have earned a considerable amount of money through the medium of the Press down the years, so I don't want to give the impression that I am biting the hand that has helped to feed me.

But although I have made a lot of marvellous friends among newspapermen, others have been right bastards.

Perhaps some of it has been my own doing. I accept that I am the sort of colourful figure they make a bee-line for, and I have the sort of outgoing nature that means I am ready made copy for any of the writers who can sense a story.

On balance, though I have enjoyed some terrific write-ups, I consider that, overall, I have had a bit of a rough deal from the Press.

It has got to the stage now where I daren't breathe the wrong way, or make even the slightest of wrong moves, without they are on my doorstep. Practically anything that happens to me nowadays is headlines.

There have been times when it has reached ridiculous proportions. I remember once when I was involved in a motoring incident and being me, it was the usual headlines, prominently displayed.

On the same page of one of those papers who splashed the story of my accident, was tucked away in a corner another story with a small headline which read something after this fashion: 'General Amin Murders Five Priests.' I ask you, which was worse?

It seems the morals in soccer are different from those in every other facet of life, though why this should be, I have no idea.

I have asked for, and deserved, a lot of my bad write-ups. But some of the media men have let me down badly at times.

I never seem to have had any real problems with the provincial football writers who seem to be closer to the game than the Fleet Street men, perhaps because they have a strong relationship with their local clubs.

I always got on well with people like David Meek, the Manchester journalist who follows United, and Neil Hallam, who does the same sort of job at Derby.

At national level, one of my best friends was the late James Connolly of the *Sunday Express*, a super man and a great journalist—someone who would never let you down in a 100 years. Peter Batt has always been fair, making sure what he could and couldn't quote simply by asking me. Hugh McIlvanney is another straight man—and of course there are others.

But many of them have used me, misquoted me, and done their favourite dirty trick on me by the old, but still widely used method of taking quotes out of context and making them appear much more damaging than they really are.

The comparatively recent fuss I got into over my alleged assertion that all managers were cheats and liars was a classic example.

The headlines were their usual size, as you can imagine. Once again it was the outrageous Doc putting his foot in it. But was it?

Strangely enough, my strongest ally on this occasion was a journalist—Denis Signy, a well-known freelance writer in the London area.

It was he who one day invited me to address a Press luncheon and of course, after the talk, there were the usual questions which I was happy to answer, as I always am.

I was QPR manager at the time and among the questions put to me after the luncheon was one of which I should have been more wary, but I tried to give my usual frank, honest answer—and the outcome was that I found myself in trouble with the Secretaries and Managers' Association.

It was a simple enough question–'Do you think managers cheat?' And I gave a simple, totally honest answer–'Yes, of course we do.' And I then gave illustrations to explain my answer.

Suppose we've got a player whom we know has got a lot of ability, but perhaps he's not doing the job for us, week in and week out, that we expect of him. We tell him he's a better player than he actually is, we might even tell him that Ron Greenwood is.at the game to watch him. This is designed to motivate him and lift him. But is it really motivation, or is it a confidence trick?

Our team is winning 2-0 with five minutes to go, and we take the ball into the corner and waste time. You can see it every Saturday. Some managers would call that gamesmanship. I, Tommy Docherty, call that cheating. Do we tell lies, I was asked. 'Of course we do, some of us–including myself,' I replied.

Someone will ring and ask our opinion of a player. If we're selling him, we say what a good player he is, and he's worth £100,000 when we know he's only worth £50,000. We might end by getting an offer of £60,000, so we've got £10,000 more than we wanted anyway. Normal business, some might say. Common sense.

To me, it's also cheating and telling lies–and I admit I've done it myself.

That's because we're trapped by the system in which we work. Many of us have to behave this way to get on and get the best out of situations. At the end of the day, if you're a manager, you're judged by your transfer deals as well as by results.

I'm not saying that instead, if we were scrupulously honest in all our statements and replies, we'd go under–that would be stretching things too far. But I'm sure we wouldn't be as successful.

The important thing as far as this Press luncheon matter was concerned is that I didn't say 'all managers are cheats and liars.' *They* suggested it with their headlines and stories.

I had been careful to point out that *some* managers cheated and lied in this way. It was part of their job.

But that made no impression on the hawks. They'd got the story they'd come for. The next day it was 'Tommy Docherty says managers are cheats and liars.' Up and down the land, they must have been saying 'Doc's done it again.'

Denis Signy is an experienced journalist so I won't say he was surprised. But he was upset because he was the one who had invited me to the luncheon as a guest. He rang me up and offered to help in any way, because he knew the quotes had been taken out of context and dressed up.

But the damage had been done, and within a few hours the Secretaries and Managers' Association were on the warpath.

And what's more, I don't think that publicity helped me in any way with my perjury case—for on the face of it, once again, here was Doc admitting telling lies.

How could I seriously make such an assertion anyway? I don't know all the managers for a start. What I was saying was that some of us did it in the framework of our jobs and because of the situation we are in, it almost becomes second nature. If you like, it's soccer wheeling and dealing.

The Association—in which there are many good friends of mine and some who aren't so friendly—took a decision not to criticise each other because they said it didn't help the image of the game.

Fair enough. But at least I'd not mentioned any specific names in my reply to the Press, and had spoken only in general terms. And the policy didn't prevent the Association criticising me, a fellow member!

I got a letter from the Association asking me to explain the remarks I made. I said that I would, and I was to meet Alan Dicks and Bill McGarry, whom they had deputed to talk to me, to do just that. But I was away the day of the arranged meeting because of a game, and couldn't make it, and I then heard that in my absence I had been fined £100.

Unless I paid by a certain date, I was told, I would be expelled from the Association.

I wrote back telling them I had no intention of paying the £100 because I had been in no position to defend myself against their suggestion that I had brought the game into disrepute. And what's more, I told them they wouldn't need to expel me, because

I could no longer remain a member of an organisation of which I considered some of the members were a bunch of hypocrites.

Which brings me back to the system. We are all guided by the situations created by that system and you would have to be a paragon of virtue always to give an honest answer when you're doing business with another manager. That's all I was saying.

I've known cases of a transfer where relevant pages of a player's medical history are removed, because the buying club would not have bought him had they known the full details of the injuries he'd received in the past.

All that sort of thing goes on and everyone in the game knows it. So why all the schemozzle when somebody ups and says it in public?

We signed a player at Derby County after the deadline. We were told by the Football League that if we slipped the letter through to them by the Friday night, things would be all right, as long as it was post-marked before 5 o'clock that evening. So we went down to the Post Office, and sent the letter off to Lytham, duly franked, so that they would receive it in their post first thing Saturday morning.

That was bending the rules, but everyone in football knows it goes on.

Some managers are very wary in their dealings with the Press, and after my sort of experience at that luncheon, can you blame them?

The writers have always known that I take the attitude that if they ask me a question, I will always try to give them an answer. I think in my job as a manager, I owe them that. We're in the entertainment business, after all.

I have found the news reporters are the worst. Some of the football writers aren't so clever, but the news reporters are nearly always the villains of the piece as far as I have been concerned.

Some of the newsmen who hounded me and Mary and pestered me around the time of the High Court case, they've been divorced, living with other women and so on. And they go on about me being the bad egg. But no one would want to read about them.

Some of the soccer writers go straight for the jugular. When it's me or Cloughie, the tone of the headlines would be 'Doc Wields the Axe' or 'Clough Drops Star Striker.' If it's say, Ron Greenwood, it's 'Greenwood's Tactical Switch.'

Of course, the old fail-safe for the football writers is their response 'We don't write the headlines.' Now I know enough about the mechanics of newspapers to know that the men who write the stories don't write the headlines. But isn't it a wonderful escape route?

Sometimes the headlines can be quite frightening and crippling – but always the writers can hold up their hands and say 'Not mine'.

Managers have also got to be on their guard against the newspapermen who make friends with the players, just to get stories from them.

The one way to stop that would be to impose a ban on players talking to the media, but I've never put that into operation because it would be fundamentally wrong.

It's a free country and I don't mind my players speaking to the Press. But I always warn the players that if they speak to the Press, and the story is printed, and it brings the club into disrepute or looks bad for them personally, I'll fine them. I tell them that when they're talking, therefore, they must bear those things in mind. Because they will be used just as I've been used in the past.

My philosophy is that the Press are a necessary evil. Now you may consider that sentiment to be a bit strong.

But I've always accepted the fact that they've a job to do. Like me, they've got families and mouths to feed, and mortgages to keep up. How they go about it sometimes is what I object to. I get annoyed when they moralise and they're probably worse than the people they're writing about.

Though I am personal friends with some pressmen, most of them you never really know. When I meet people, I am open with them, and I like them to be open with me. I'll give stories to them for nothing. I always try to be civil to working journalists.

And I have never objected to criticism of me as a manager – tactically, I mean. They have their opinions, and they're entitled to them.

Some managers take the view that football writers aren't in a position to criticise because they've never played the professional game. I don't go along with that. You could say, by that token, that a few managers haven't the right to be in their jobs because they've never played the game at top level.

Lawrie McMenemy didn't play soccer at high level – but what a manager. Tony Waddington didn't, nor Bertie Mee.

I think I could do a journalist's job. I wouldn't have to adapt – I could go to a paper tomorrow and be a great journalist because I'm a ferret and I'd get the news. Len Shackleton, Jackie Milburn, the late Sam Bartram, Jimmy Armfield ... they've all done it. I don't think it's a particularly hard job ...

What I really laugh about with the media is how some of them set themselves as experts on a number of sports. They report on soccer. They say Kevin Keegan did this wrong, and George Best did that wrong; the next day, they're on boxing, saying Muhammad Ali's slowing down, and his left's a bit weak; then they're at Wimbledon saying that if Bjorn Borg had played his ground strokes a bit better, he'd have won more easily; then they're up at the golf telling Jack Nicklaus where he's going wrong.

They're masters of everything. It wouldn't be so bad if they were masters of one sport. They don't have to have played it to write about it. But to tell the performers where they're going wrong as if they know it all, that makes me smile.

And those amazing tags that their newspapers give them! 'The No. 1 sportswriter' – who says so?

You get 'The Writer the Players Trust' and 'The Players' Friend' – have all the players said so? – and 'The Man in the Know' and suchlike.

Of course, I accept that there's good and bad in every walk of life. And for every supposed big man with an undeserved tag, there are dozens of good, honest hard-working writers outside Fleet Street.

I found them in Australia. Curiously when I was 'down under' in 1964, they were terrible to me. In 1980, when I went to coach Sydney Olympic, they were all marvellous. They actually asked me if I minded whether they criticised me, tactically speaking.

'Of course, I don't,' I replied. 'That's your job – go ahead.'

I'm an extrovert and being in the public eye, I seem to attract the Press guys like flies. But I cannot change at my time in life, and I don't see why I should. All I have ever asked is for people to take me as they find me.

That means inevitably that anything I do that is slightly off-centre, it's a story. Someone once said I'd figured almost as many times on the front pages as I have on the back. Maybe that's true.

I know one thing. With all the publicity I've been given down the years, I'd never again go to court of my own choice.

I was in court when I was a kid in Glasgow through pinching apples and kicking a football in the street. I reckon I did more wrong then than anything concerned with my perjury case.

With all the things going on around us in the world today – terrorism, rioting, looting, murder and so on – I reckon that what I've done wrong is way down in the priority list of shame.

So I say by and large, I've had a raw deal from the Press. But things will be just the same, and this won't affect my attitude towards them.

Because if you ask anybody who knows me well, they'll confirm that the way I see the great scheme of things is this: life's too sweet, and too short, to bear grudges and hold vendettas. What's happened has happened. Let's get on with the game.

# 10
# Derby County – and the Police Probe

I'VE HAD a few shocks and surprises in my life. But none of them matches up to what happened one morning during my second spell as manager of Queen's Park Rangers.

I was lying in my bed at the Kensington Hilton hotel when there came a knock on the door of my room.

Standing on the threshold were police from Derby. 'Are you Mr Docherty?' they asked. 'Yes,' I replied.

'You'll have to come with us,' they said.

I asked if I could ring Mary, but they said no, I had to go with them immediately. They arrested me and took me straight to Derby in a car.

I was allowed to contact my solicitor then, and he soon arrived at the police station. So did Mary, shortly after I telephoned her – and she was expecting our baby at the time.

Before that the police had told me they were making enquiries into alleged irregularities with players going to the United States, and any involvement I may have had in that.

'Before you start,' I said to the police inspector at Derby, 'you're wasting your time, and the public's money.'

And I emphatically declared that I, and Stuart Webb, the Derby County secretary at the time, had done nothing wrong. When my solicitor arrived, that was the start of a nine-hour interrogation.

It had taken the police six months to get around to interviewing me. The investigation had started when police met the Derby County party returning from a trip to Majorca.

I believe it was instigated by two members of the Derby board.

Stuart Webb had been on the trip, and the next thing he knew was that his office was being searched for what might prove to be irregularities in the club's finances.

After that, all I knew was what I read in the newspapers, and the enquiries dragged on and on. Until that day in the hotel...

At the police station, they asked me why I gave Donald O'Riordan—who is ironically now at Preston with me—a free transfer, when a year later another club paid £30,000 for him.

I told them the club gave O'Riordan a free transfer on my recommendation, after which he went to Tulsa Roughnecks. Later, Preston paid a fee for him and he came back to England.

I answered the question, despite the concern of my solicitor, because I had nothing to hide.

Then, of course, I had to explain to the police something they probably wouldn't realise, but which people in the game—and even some followers—would understand without explanation.

'We gave him a free,' I explained, 'because like all the clubs, we were pruning our staff, and the players I had were better than the one we were releasing. It was done at that stage of the season rather than at the end, because then a lot of players would be given frees, and would be scrambling to find new clubs.'

And I told the inspector: 'What you may not realise, inspector, is that then Donald O'Riordan could go to any club he wished.'

I could spot the inference, which was that somehow I had made something out of the transaction. But all I was interested in was in cutting down my staff.

Now I know the police later went to see Nobby Stiles, who was then the Preston manager, and asked him why he bought a player from Tulsa for £30,000 when Tommy Docherty had given him a free transfer. I can imagine Nobby's frame of mind as he tried to explain the mechanics of soccer transfers to laymen.

Nobby told them 'That sort of thing is happening all the time'. And as anyone who knows anything about soccer will verify, that's exactly true.

Look at Steve Daley. Malcolm Allison spent £1,350,000 on him from Wolves and later on he was sold for £300,000. John Blackley went from Hibernian to Newcastle for £100,000–and a few months later, they gave him a free.

The police were looking for things that in reality weren't there. They then mentioned the case of Gerry Daly, who went from Derby to the Boston Teamen on loan for a fee of £25,000 per year. 'What did you get out of this?' they asked me.

'The only people who got anything out of it,' I replied, 'were Derby, who got a total £75,000 for three years, and Gerry Daly, who got the best of both worlds, playing for Derby in our season and Boston in theirs. I got nothing, neither did I expect to get anything.'

And I further explained to the police that any transfers were always conducted in conjunction with the club's board of directors, and not arranged just by the manager.

So my interrogation ended. And the enquiries went slowly on. The police went all over the place, interviewing people in the game. They went to America–but nothing came of it. That's not surprising because as I told the police in the first instance, it was a glorious and expensive waste of time.

All the police got out of it was a few good holidays in the States. All I got was a nine-hour grilling–and they can be pretty intimidating people.

There were two aggravating consequences of that police investigation as far as I was concerned. One was that it cost me another £3,000 in legal fees while they were making the enquiries. The other was that Stuart Webb left Derby County. He was a superb secretary, and a commercially great PRO. Now he's no longer in football.

Until such time as it was all cleared up, there was always that stigma there at Derby that there could be something at the back of it.

The enquiry was a total waste of time, and it was a pity that the people who instigated the investigation didn't suffer as well.

In my opinion, they wanted George Hardy–the chairman at the time–out of the club.

To this day, mud sticks to myself from that investigation. That was why I was delighted when Preston took me on this summer.

They did their homework.

When a club which has a gentleman like Tom Finney as president is prepared to take me on, that's a big compliment, and it makes me proud. I'm grateful to Preston for giving me the opportunity to come back into League soccer.

I was at the Baseball Ground for a little over 18 months, and I'd have been quite happy to stay on if Queen's Park Rangers had not come in for me in April 1979. But all the time I was there, a ferment of disagreement at board level existed – a power struggle in which the directors seemed trying to cut each other's throats.

It reminded me of the situation which I'd found at Villa Park in the old days and which happily now seems to have changed for the better, which must be great for Ron Saunders. I know how he must have felt trying to work with all that argument going on around him.

I'd been away from Old Trafford only a couple of months when I got the Derby job. An old friend of mine, Tom Pendry, the Labour MP for Stalybridge, was instrumental in the negotiations which led up to it, and I actually clinched the job at a meeting at Tom's house, which is just down the road from my own home in the village of Charlesworth in Derbyshire.

Tom is a Derby 'fanatic', his wife is a Derby girl, and they were delighted. So was I. The early days were very interesting.

It suited me very well because it wasn't far from my home. And the crowd were responsive to me and the team.

I have sometimes been asked whether the 'ghost' of Brian Clough walked the corridors of the Baseball Ground and I can categorically say the knowledge that he had been there before me and had done such a great job, never bothered me in the slightest.

I'm as big in the game as Cloughie if not bigger. I'm a good friend of his, and of Peter Taylor – I like them. And we've always got on well.

In some ways, the situation facing me was similar to that at Old Trafford. There were some great players at County, but they were getting old. And the message was 'Come in Tom and weed them out'. And the chairman, George Hardy, was going to do a lot of great things for the club.

One of the problems was that there was no money to spend. You had to sell a player to raise the cash to buy one. Despite this, according to George Hardy, I was going to be the first manager in the Football League to run a Rolls Royce! Needless to say that was a pipe-dream.

There were those on the board who wanted George Hardy out so he was under pressure from them. And instead of being a strong chairman, which he should have been, he succumbed to them.

I took Mr Hardy once to a dinner in Manchester to meet Peter Swales, the Manchester City chairman. Peter gave him the insight on how to be a successful chairman—to be strong and powerful and run the club with the aid of the manager and the secretary. But it was a waste of time.

All the time there was this in-fighting going on in the board room. One of the things I soon found myself up against was this silly 'rule' of the board's that no player must be sold to Nottingham Forest. Or what it really meant, no player must be sold to Brian Clough.

My guess is that the Derby board realised that they slipped up in the first place by letting Clough and Taylor leave the Baseball Ground. And they weren't prepared to see Clough succeed with ex-Derby players.

When they found they needed a manager they brought in Dave Mackay. He did a good job, though he may have found himself in Cloughie's shadow a little.

That wasn't my experience, and in fairness to Cloughie, I never saw his name splattered all over the Derby newspaper while I was there.

Though Brian had done a fantastic job for Derby, the directors were not happy at his success later. At one time Sam Longson, who was chairman at Derby in Clough's time, said he looked upon him as a son. Then things changed ... but it wasn't Cloughie's fault.

I could understand why Brian hardly ever went to board meetings at Derby, because while I was there I found it difficult to get any sense out of them.

There was one director who used to snoop about the dressing-rooms and the kitchens. He'd go into the kitchen and say to the woman in charge 'I see you've got an extra bottle of brandy–where did you get that from?' and that sort of thing. It was like having a spy walking around.

Sam Longson used to ask the players for complimentary tickets for his friends.

I liked Bob Innes, the vice-chairman, and in a way I liked George. But he talked big and did very little.

When he was ousted from the chairman's position, I rang him and said 'I told you this would happen–you should have been stronger. How you were ever successful in business, I'll never know.'

All right, I was blunt, but all this sort of thing was no good for Derby County and not so hot for the fans who knew from the local paper this backroom feuding was going on.

Mr Moore, who is now the chairman, is too concerned with finances in my opinion, and I sometimes wonder if he would rather see Derby in the Fourth Division with one million pounds in the bank, than in the First Division while £250 in the red. He is an accountant, and I told him once that he knew the price of everything and the value of nothing.

Anyway, these are the sort of people Cloughie eventually decided he couldn't work with. I must say I sympathise.

I clashed with the board when I wanted to sell Charlie George to Forest. But Archie Gemmill, who had been a good player under Clough, joined him at Forest and did well there too. After that, the board decided to block any players going to the City Ground.

It wasn't a case of not wishing to sell a player to Forest, as a club. It was a case of not wanting to do anything that might help Cloughie to be more successful. That's daft because if a club wants to buy a player–and in that particular case, Forest wanted Charlie George–their money is as good as anyone else's.

Nevertheless, despite all this boardroom atmosphere, I quite enjoyed my spell at Derby and I was looking forward to seeing my contract through with about another 18 months to run.

But at a time when the results were going too well, I could see which way the wind was blowing, after Mr Hardy—who was then still chairman—had an extraordinary conversation with myself, my No. 2 Frank Blunstone, and my chief scout Gordon Clayton.

It was in a restaurant and Mr Hardy, who had been sitting with some friends, came over. I thought he'd had a drink or two. And in front of me, he asked Frank and Gordon: 'If Tom got the sack, tomorrow, what would you two do?'

Frank told him: 'I think you're out of order talking like that, Mr Chairman.' And I intervened. I said to Hardy: 'If I got the sack tomorrow, Frank and Gordon would stay at Derby County, because they're under contract and they've got families.'

The only reason I can think of for this incredible lack of diplomacy is that if Frank and Gordon had said they'd leave in that circumstance, Hardy would have realised he'd be without any staff to run the club, so he'd better leave things as they were. Other than that, who knows? Incidentally, they sacked Frank later.

There was another remarkable incident when Derby were in danger of relegation from the First Division, and so were Queen's Park Rangers. QPR were playing at Leeds knowing that if they lost they would go down, and we would stay up. That's what happened.

Five of the six Derby directors went to Elland Road to see the match! The QPR directors in the Leeds boardroom afterwards must have thought 'What are they all doing here?' My own name for the Derby board was 'The Crazy Gang'.

Within a short while, ironically, in came QPR for me. And I think the Derby board weren't sorry. They could see me becoming strong there—and they wouldn't have liked that. I think they really want a yes-man.

So I was on my way back to Shepherd's Bush and to Jim Gregory. Life hadn't been dull at Derby—and it certainly wasn't going to be dull working again under a man like Jim...

# 11
# Turbulent Times at QPR

I SACKED Queen's Park Rangers once and they later sacked me twice. But though the moods of the chairman Jim Gregory were like the English weather – they changed every day – and we had some right ding-dong rows and differences, there is much I admire about him.

Jim is different from other chairmen in that QPR is his club. He actually owns it. And because of that, he doesn't mess around with such things as board meetings. I think all the time I was there in my second spell, he called only three – and two of those were cancelled!

My first experience at Loftus Road lasted 28 days and was one of the soccer sensations of the age. Even in a game used to the comings and goings of managers like passengers at a railway station, this was a bit unusual.

I had a rough sort of understanding with Jim when I was appointed in November 1968. But the powers you think you have got when you arrive are often very different from the powers you find you have got later!

And the very first time I wanted to buy a player, I realised that things weren't going to work out. In fact, after 48 hours, I'd sussed out the lie of the land and knew it wouldn't last.

I wanted to buy a player called Brian Tiler from Rotherham, the club I'd just left. He would have done a good job for QPR at that time. But that was when I first realised that Jim Gregory only permits his managers to buy players if *he* approves of them also.

It doesn't matter how much his manager wants the player – he's got to like him too, otherwise there's no deal. At least that was how it was then. So I had no alternative but to call it quits straight-away. For I'm no yes-man and never will be.

I tried to contact Jim but he was away on a health farm. He always was when you couldn't find him. Eventually I managed to get him on the telephone and told him there was no point in me going on. 'You're joking?' he half asked. 'I'm not–I'm deadly serious.' He was amazed and embarrassed. So I walked out.

But there must have been something about me that Jim liked for over 10 years later he called me back again–and this time things lasted a little longer, though he did sack me twice afterwards. Perhaps that was his way of getting his own back for what I had done in walking out the first time!

It was May 1979 and he had just fired Steve Burtenshaw and needed a manager quickly. He approached Derby for permission to speak to me, received it, and we soon reached agreement.

I knew there had been lots of upheaval at QPR. There always will be–it's that sort of one-man club.

We'd both been to blame for what happened 10 years earlier. The first thing he said to me was 'I've changed since the last time we knew each other,' and I replied 'So have I. We didn't give it a real chance.'

He assured me: 'If it doesn't work out this time between you and me, Tom, I'll have to pack it in.'

When I went to work for Jim Gregory the second time, I knew where I stood. It would have been no use moaning and groaning about it afterwards–he'll never change. A leopard never changes its spots. But it was a great experience working with him–one which I would never had missed.

I reckon if a lot of managers were able to work for six months under Jim, they'd be better for it, because they'd learn a lot about wheeling and dealing and negotiating.

So when I found myself back in London, I knew exactly what I was letting myself in for once again.

I had to pick up, mentally, a team which had been relegated to the Second Division, and looking at them, I couldn't say I was

surprised at their fate. They'd sold Phil Parkes, a first-rate goalkeeper, to West Ham, and because of relegation, one or two of the
other players weren't keen on staying.

There were some good kids there, because the club's youth
scheme was a good one and very productive. We went on a
four-match tour of Nigeria which gave me a chance to assess
things and prepare for the new season.

We brought in Clive Allen and Paul Goddard, and when we
started the new term, we'd got together a great young side.

We finished up four points the wrong side of promotion, and I
always said that but for my unfortunate incident with the
hooligans at Stockport railway station, which I shall relate in
detail later, we would have gone up. For while I was away in
hospital recovering for six weeks, we picked up only two points out
of twelve.

One of my better buys was Tony Currie, and two other great
influences in the side were Stan Bowles and Don Shanks.

The Press always gave the impression that these were the 'bad
boys' but that wasn't the case as far as I was concerned. You
couldn't get three nicer lads.

I never had any bother with Stan Bowles—he never caused me a
minute's worry. They used to rattle on about his gambling—but it
was his money and he was entitled to do what he liked with it.

He was supposed to be always late. But he was never late
for me. On away trips, he'd say to me 'All right if I go to the
dogs, Boss?' I'd say: 'That's okay Stan, be in by eleven.' And
he was.

Stan later went to Forest but I could never see that working out.
Maybe Brian handled him differently from me.

At the end of the season, however, Jim made a surprise move.
He announced that I'd been sacked. The players were up in arms,
protesting about this step. I think that, at the time, Jim would
have preferred Terry Venables as manager.

I was heartened by the players' support for me, for we'd worked
well together and only missed out on promotion by a small
margin. Jim climbed down, said there had been a mistake, and
re-instated me.

But all the time that summer, things were getting closer and closer to the appointment of Venables at Loftus Road.

Looking back, it was quite an amusing conversation when Jim brought up the subject of us parting company. 'Well, Tom,' he said, 'I'm thinking of calling it a day.' And tongue-in-cheek, I replied: 'I wouldn't do that, chairman – I think you're doing a good job.' He had a sense of humour and even he could see the funny side of that one.

However, he was serious. He meant me. He said I was a part-time manager. 'You're never here,' he said, referring to the fact that my home was still in the north and that I was doing a lot of commuting.

'I'm here every day for training, here most days until five o'clock, and I go to watch games,' I told him. 'I'm doing my job.'

'You haven't got a house down here yet,' he said. 'That's because I can't afford one,' I answered.

I turned the conversation around. 'If we'd won promotion, you wouldn't be sacking me.' 'Yes, I would,' he replied. I thought that's nice. But on reflection, he probably would have, for it is his club, he does what he likes. To be honest, if it was all my money, I'd do exactly the same. He has always put his money where his mouth is. Besides, I suspected he wanted Terry.

He'd been quite happy about my 'living away' situation while we were top of the Second Division, and in fact, I had always wanted to move down to London providing the house was right.

He actually offered me the use of a house, rent-free, for a year. It was a nice gesture, and I told him I appreciated it. But I wanted Mary to see it first, because it would have been no good to us if she hadn't liked it, or the area it was in. That didn't go down well, and two months later when I saw another house £10,000 cheaper than the other one he'd offered, he wouldn't help us with that.

You see, Jim's a man of whims. Terry must have found this out by now. They'll do well together – but they won't get much sleep. And in the long run, their relationship won't work out.

I think Jim rated Terry highly as a manager. He'd been a good player at QPR. I also think Jim could see a lot of himself in Terry.

Terry is always referred to as one of the country's up-and-coming managers, but apart from taking Palace into the First Division, what's he ever done? Having got them there, he got out.

But I always give Jim Gregory his due in terms of what he has done for QPR. No one else could have done it. Look at the stadium now compared to the old days – and it's all been down to him.

He makes the decisions. He's got through a lot of managers, but so have a lot of other clubs.

Towards the end of my time at Loftus Road, in fact I think during my last few days there, I recall having a conversation with Jim about Terry, at a stage when he must have been virtually certain in his own mind that Venables was the man he was after to take over from me.

Terry had been to one of our games, and I'd joked with him: 'Hello, Terry – spying again?' Terry laughed and went on his way. 'A great lad, Terry,' Jim said to me. I was a little uncomplimentary, however, and Jim clearly didn't like it.

'He's a rubber-dinghy man,' I said. And I wasn't talking behind Terry's back – he knows what I think of him, because I told him to his face, 'You're a rubber-dinghy man.'

When the boat's sinking, Terry will get out and look after No. 1.

The 1980-81 season had barely begun before I was in the headlines once more, this time over the Andy Ritchie transfer. And it caused a hell of a fuss with my old club Chelsea. It proved to be the touch-paper for the fuse which burned its way towards my second, and final dismissal.

Andy Ritchie and his father are good friends of mine. I signed the lad when I was at United. And we agreed terms to buy Andy for QPR. Jim Gregory actually did the spadework, as he sometimes did in affairs of money and buying players – he was brilliant at it.

Dave Sexton promised him he'd sell Andy to us, and Jim told me 'Fly up to Manchester, Tom, the deal's on'.

The next morning, I went up, went to the airport hotel to meet Dave, but I got a phone call telling me he had changed his mind.

Apparently he considered he'd sold too many players to me.

I gave him a bit of a slating through the columns of the Press, saying that he couldn't make up his mind, he wasn't a man of decision, and so on. Jim didn't like that because he's always thought a lot of Dave, who of course was a manager under him previously.

The next thing I read was that Brighton had agreed terms with Andy, and at this point, I told the Press we should get a chance to get back into the bidding. They told me that Chelsea were also interested, and that's when the storm broke.

'If I was Andy,' I told the Press, 'if I had the choice of a First or a Second Division club, I'd pick the First Division club. Because Andy's a First Division player.'

Within hours, the papers had done it on me again. 'Docherty Tells Ritchie: Don't Go to Chelsea,' blared the headlines. Jim was on to me soon. Brian Mears and Geoff Hurst had reacted from Chelsea, telephoned him and said they were livid, and that Andy might have gone to Chelsea if I hadn't made those remarks.

But there was no way Andy would have gone to Chelsea. The only Second Division club Andy would have gone to was QPR–because of me.

That rankled with Jim also, and things built up to a point between us where I guessed it would blow wide open. There was some sort of apology conjured up for Chelsea, I was fired–and Andy Ritchie went to Brighton, a First Division club.

When it happened, I thought to myself: well, now I'm out of work again, I've got the perjury case coming up some time, nobody will be prepared to take me on until that's over and done with.

I might have known the offers are always forthcoming for a man of experience. In the space of a few days, I found myself on the way to Australia. I was out of the country for a whole season working 'down under' with Sydney Olympic but I found I missed the big scene. I knew it wouldn't be long before I was back in some capacity or other.

# 12
# Docherty the Player

TWENTY YEARS have passed since I finished my playing career—a career in which I wore the colours of three great clubs and appeared for my country 25 times.

When I look back upon it now, it not only seems a bit like a bygone age, but compared to the ups and downs of my managerial life, it was like a placid lake beside a broiling ocean.

Two men shaped my early destiny and I shall never forget their contributions in my life. One of them was one of the most famous names in British soccer history—the coach Jimmy Hogan. The other wasn't famous, but to me he was a saintly man. He was Father Joseph Connolly, a Catholic priest where I grew up in the Glasgow slums and without his help and inspiration during my childhood, I don't know how we would have fared.

Rags to riches is the fairy-story stuff which makes for good films and best-selling novels. Well, whatever riches I have earned from football seem largely to have blown away downwind. And as for the rags, I can vouch for their authenticity.

I make no apologies for referring at this stage to my poor background, not because I want any sympathy, but simply because it may enable you to understand why my driving ambition in life was to become successful.

It was so that my family would never have to go through the squalor which I faced as a child or endure the sort of heroic attempts of my father and mother to rise above the awful conditions so many of us lived under in those days in the notorious Gorbals district of Glasgow.

My father I never really got to know. He worked in an iron

factory and died when I was only nine. My recollection is that he rarely seemed to be well.

Somehow we eked out an existence, he and my mother and my two sisters. We lived in a 'single end', as it was known, and life was grim. I didn't get a new suit until I was 15 and any football boots I was able to wear were always cast-offs from other people.

Father Connolly helped us to keep going. He came in to see us most days and I thought he was such a wonderful man that I determined to hand over an entire week's wages to him one day, which I eventually did. It was the princely sum of 25s 9d.

Round about this time my football life had begun. My mother came to watch me play for St Paul's Boys' Guild, and much to my surprise I was asked to join a team called Shettleston Juniors, who gave me half-a-crown travelling expenses each time I turned out. It was a humble start—but I was on my way.

National Service may have been a bind to many, but to me it came like a merciful release from all the pitiful conditions I had known up to that point. It taught me self-reliance and discipline, and maybe this is why as a manager I have demanded these sort of qualities from my players.

I went to Palestine with the Highland Light Infantry. At the same time, my football was now taking shape. Playing alongside other Army men like Arthur Rowley, the burly man who went on to become the Football League's most prolific goalscorer, Adam Little of Rangers, Frank McCue and Ken Bowyer of Stoke, did me no harm, and I played for the Army representative side, which was my first real honour.

When I was demobbed after two years abroad, I was somewhat surprised to hear that Glasgow Celtic were showing an interest in me. You couldn't get me to the desk quick enough to sign the forms. For a Catholic in Glasgow who was desperate for a career in soccer, what better break could there have been?

My wages were £9 in season, and £7 in the close-season. That seems ridiculous by today's standards when players collect many thousands of pounds just for signing on. But to me it sounded great, and it was very good money compared with Army pay.

It was during a spell of special training that I met my future wife Agnes.

It was ironic that I should now be playing for Celtic, because when I was a lad I could never afford to watch them play. Sometimes I whipped into the ground 20 minutes from the end when they opened the gates up for early-leavers.

The man barring my path to a regular first-team spot was one of the Scottish all-time greats, Bobby Evans, a dynamic wing-half of tremendous vitality. The only time I seemed to be able to get into the side was when he was away playing for Scotland, or on the injured list!

At this time there was paper talk that Preston were keen on me, and it suddenly turned into something when the Celtic manager, Jim McGrory, asked me if I would be interested in a move to Lancashire.

The bait was tempting—£10 all year round and a club house. Agnes and I were planning to get married, so I signed. I received a present of £750 from Celtic, and considering I had made only a dozen or so first-team appearances, I thought that was generous.

But I contemplated Jimmy Hogan's influence in those Celtic days and how much his shrewdness and foresight had given me a shove in the right direction. For Jimmy first saw me playing at outside-left and told McGrory: 'That boy will be a great player and he'll play for Scotland one day. But not as a winger—he's a born wing-half.'

Nevertheless, Preston insisted on my turning out as a winger after I had joined them in November, 1949 and that's where I played in the first few weeks in the reserve side. Even when I made my first-team debut—and with it my first senior appearance in English football—on Christmas Day, it was on the wing.

Of course, by this time I was in awe of one of our players who to this day sits only a few yards away from me in those same stands in front of which we played so many games together—Tom Finney.

Tom was something special in talent and temperament, and although he was one of the finest wingers the game has ever known, later in his career he played at centre-forward with real distinction, although he was only slightly built for that position.

I never heard him complain at rough tackling, or tick a team-mate off. He was not only the perfect player – and that's a description I don't use lightly – he was the perfect gentleman. No wonder he commands the respect he does, even to this day, when he is now the Preston club president.

Another man I learned a lot from during those nine years I served at Deepdale was Cliff Britton, my manager who had been an England player and was a member of what many regarded as the finest half-back line ever to play for England – Britton, Stan Cullis and Joe Mercer.

A couple of seasons after I joined North End we won promotion back to the First Division. In all, I chalked up 325 League appearances and I missed few matches during those nine years.

The only serious injury I had was a broken ankle, but because I kept myself very fit, I was back from that in double-quick time to play at Wembley in the Cup Final against West Bromwich Albion in 1954. But the dream became something of a nightmare. Tom Finney had an off day, I gave away a penalty, and we lost 3-2.

Tom was bottled up by sheer weight of numbers and everywhere he went there seemed to be three Albion men barring the route to goal. I did supply the pass for Charlie Wayman to score one of our goals but the penalty dismayed me.

I always maintained that Ray Barlow, the big Albion half-back, collided with me and that the worst that should have been given against me was an indirect free kick. But the referee Arthur Luty – a very fine ref, incidentally – reckoned later I didn't intend to play the ball. His version was the only important one, of course, and Ronnie Allen scored. But not without some of the most nerve-racking moments he and I have ever experienced.

First the ball rolled off the penalty spot. Then Willie Cunningham, our Scottish full-back, pointed out that it was still not placed correctly – another delay. When Ronnie finally took the kick the ball seemed to hit a hole on the spot, and didn't go true.

It struck our goalkeeper George Thompson on the right arm and was deflected into the net. At the other end the photographers got a classic picture of Jim Sanders, the Albion goalkeeper, turning the other way because he couldn't bear to watch.

So that was that. It was the only Cup Final I played in, and even when I went there 13 years later as Chelsea manager, I still finished on the losing side! Such are the fates.

I suppose the good years couldn't go on for ever before there came some blot on the horizon and it arrived in 1958 when there was a rift between me and the Preston club over my international responsibilities.

Preston had arranged a tour of South Africa for six weeks at the time that Scotland were competing in the World Cup Finals in Sweden.

To me, playing in the World Cup finals was something that couldn't be missed – the chance of a lifetime. But North End didn't see it quite the same way. They said I couldn't go to Sweden, even though I could have joined them later in South Africa. Cliff Britton dug his heels in, but I was determined and off I went to Sweden, thinking 'hang the consequences'.

Scotland played three games against Yugoslavia, Paraguay and France and lost two of them, and I didn't even get a game. Talk about frustration. But before I had left for Sweden, Preston's attitude had so upset me that I was determined to put in a transfer request as soon as I arrived home. And I did.

The club did try to dissuade me, but to no avail. So for the first match of the 1958-59 season against Arsenal at Deepdale, they figured there was no point in me having a first-team place if I was on the list.

The young man who took my place that day went on to become an England player and a First Division manager. His name was Gordon Milne, the son of Jimmy Milne who gave Preston such wonderful service for so many years.

So the three holders of that shirt in the Preston side in succession were Bill Shankly, myself and Gordon – all internationals and all men who went on to manage big clubs.

After that opening game Cliff Britton made one final attempt to change my mind. 'No, I must be away,' I replied. 'In that case,' he said obviously having tested me out, 'go and see George Swindin in my office.'

George was the Arsenal manager and their former goalkeeper.

It took only a few moments for me to sign for Arsenal for a fee of £27,000 – that was £25,000 more than Preston had paid Celtic for me nine years previously. I was so much in a hurry to sign for the Gunners, I clean forgot to ask what wage I would be on! Can you see players doing that today?

By this time I was an established international and had already played 22 times for Scotland. But I was to get only three more caps during my time at Highbury.

I'll always remember clearly my debut for Arsenal. It was on 27 August 1958 against Burnley, a club I have admired for so many years, and the one I persuaded my son Michael to play for when he was 16. It was a decision I never regretted and Michael went on to enjoy his career at Turf Moor under Jimmy Adamson and that old warhorse Bob Lord, who despite ruffling more than a few feathers over the years, has done a lot for soccer.

The Highbury fans had obviously not been used to a chatterbox before. This was one of my traits, I'm afraid. I would always shout, call and egg my team-mates on. The fans initially told me to belt up, but as we won that game 3-0 and I scored one, by the end of the match they had got used to me and I was cheered off.

My rabbiting during a game never got me into trouble on the field. But I once found big trouble off the field, and it taught me a lesson while I played – don't get stroppy with a referee.

I'm afraid I didn't continue that policy in my time as a manager, as you will know. But the only thing I will say in mitigation is that the pressures are a little different!

It was after an Arsenal away match that I had a go at Ken Stokes, informing him that he was a 'homer'. When the FA got his report, it mentioned that I had used foul language. I denied this but the outcome was that I was suspended for 14 days.

This was a stiff sentence at that time and it cost me about £50 in wages as well, so it was a sobering experience for me. And all because of a bit of hot-headedness on my part.

Anyway, the Highbury crowd didn't seem too worried about violence of the tongue, as Jimmy Hill used to call it. When I emerged from my suspension to play in a Cup replay against

Colchester, there was a 62,000 crowd and they cheered every time I touched the ball!

Looking back 20 years and comparing standards of refereeing today with those at that time, I would say on balance that they were better then. I think there was a lot more respect for referees in those days. I found that almost without exception, refs would make their mark early in a match, and let you know who the boss was.

There was also a sense of humour and camaraderie between players and referees. For example, if you were pulled up for a foul, and questioned it with some strong language, you'd get strong language back. Nowadays you'll be in the book for that.

The number of times I've heard refs in the old days say: 'Bugger off. Be quiet, and get on with the game.'

Players are more on edge today than they were in my time on the field, because the pressures and rewards are greater. European competition has been partly responsible for this. Naturally it has tended to make the players more tense in the pressure-cooker atmosphere, reacting far more quickly to referees' decisions.

This makes it harder for the refs, with the 'win at all costs' attitude prevailing. Refs today are hamstrung by not being allowed to use their common sense—the chief attribute they were able to manipulate when I was playing.

They will tell you themselves today: 'If I don't referee in line with all the instructions that come out from the Football League, I'll be off the list.'

Even so, I think there was more general respect for refs in my time. For one thing, the gulf between what they earned and what we earned was nowhere near as great as it is today, when they get a few quid and players get hundreds.

I was always sad that during the time I played for Scotland, they had a lot of good players, but never a team consistent enough to achieve things. We have a great togetherness as a nation, we Scots, but when it comes down to doing something, we're inclined to tackle it individually, and I think that is reflected in the approach the Scotland side had adopted down the years.

Scotland have done better than England in recent World Cups

and have actually qualified for the finals in Germany and Argentina while England have stayed at home wondering why they weren't there. But Scotland having got there, there was something lacking.

MY INTERNATIONAL RECORD FOR SCOTLAND

*With Preston*

| | | | | | |
|---|---|---|---|---|---|
| 28 Nov | 1951 | v Wales | Hampden Park | L | 0-1 |
| 18 April | 1953 | v England | Wembley | D | 2-2 |
| 6 May | 1953 | v Sweden | Hampden Park | L | 1-2 |
| 5 May | 1954 | v Norway | Hampden Park | W | 1-0 |
| 19 May | 1954 | v Norway | Oslo | D | 1-1 |
| 16 June | 1954 | v Austria | Zurich | L | 0-1 (World Cup) |
| 19 June | 1954 | v Uruguay | Basle | L | 0-7 (World Cup) |
| 16 Oct | 1954 | v Wales | Cardiff | W | 1-0 |
| 8 Dec | 1954 | v Hungary | Hampden Park | L | 2-4 |
| 2 April | 1955 | v England | Wembley | L | 2-7 (scored one) |
| 19 May | 1955 | v Austria | Vienna | W | 4-1 |
| 29 May | 1955 | v Hungary | Budapest | L | 1-3 |
| 21 Nov | 1956 | v Yugoslavia | Hampden Park | W | 2-0 |
| 6 April | 1957 | v England | Wembley | L | 1-2 |
| 8 May | 1957 | v Spain | Hampden Park | W | 4-2 (World Cup) |
| 19 May | 1957 | v Switzerland | Basle | W | 2-1 (World Cup) |
| 22 May | 1957 | v West Germany | Stuttgart | W | 3-1 |
| 26 May | 1957 | v Spain | Madrid | L | 1-4 (World Cup) |
| 5 Oct | 1957 | v Northern Ireland | Belfast | D | 1-1 |
| 6 Nov | 1957 | v Switzerland | Hampden Park | W | 3-2 (World Cup) |
| 13 Nov | 1957 | v Wales | Hampden Park | D | 1-1 |
| 19 April | 1958 | v England | Hampden Park | L | 0-4 |

*With Arsenal*

| | | | | | |
|---|---|---|---|---|---|
| 18 Oct | 1958 | v Wales | Cardiff | W | 3-0 |
| 5 Nov | 1958 | v Northern Ireland | Hampden Park | D | 2-2 |
| 11 April | 1959 | v England | Wembley | L | 0-1 |

I think that if the World Cup finals are ever staged in Scotland, they'd stand a very good chance of winning it. For I believe that the main reason England won it in 1966 was because it was staged at Wembley.

I played alongside some of the greatest players ever to pull on the dark blue–Dave Mackay, Bobby Collins, Denis Law, Jackie Mudie, George Young and so on. Yet our results were always in fits and starts. Perhaps one day Scotland will put it all together and all that natural talent will be successfully blended.

Playing football has taken me to many countries which I would never otherwise have visited and this has given me a first-rate insight into life and the football business.

One of the few places I haven't been to is Russia–and I've got no intentions of going there.

We went to Switzerland every year when I was with Preston–it was almost like a second home. Poland, Portugal, Norway, Sweden, Italy, Yugoslavia, Denmark–I've seen them all. And the United States, but I didn't fancy that. Too much razzmatazz for my liking. But I do enjoy going to Dublin. They love their football over there and the Irish are so friendly.

I also can't speak too highly of Australia, though I was there mostly as a manager with Chelsea and Manchester United, before going there for a longer spell to work for Sydney Olympic. It's a great country with a healthy future in soccer.

I had three seasons at Highbury and enjoyed every minute of it, though the closest we got to achieving anything was to finish in third place in 1958-59. In 1960 I began to feel I was losing my zest for playing and was leaning towards my long term aim of trying to reach the top as a coach and manager.

I could have joined Blackpool, but I figured if I was going to finish my playing days, I would like them to be at Highbury.

But then came the offer to move across London to Chelsea. My dream of being a coach to a big club had materialised.

I was at my own soccer crossroads. The path I would take from then on would be full of pitfalls, but always stimulating...

# 13
# My First Managerial Mountain

FACING YOUR first job as a coach or a manager can be something akin to a non-swimmer being thrown in at the deep end without a lifejacket. At least that's how I felt when I decided it was time to hang up my boots and I was confronted with my first mountain which went by the name of Chelsea Football Club.

The first two conversations I had were enough to put a timid man off for life. The manager Ted Drake told me he'd much rather have had Vic Buckingham as his coach. I'd hardly got over that blow to my dignity when the chairman Joe Mears commented: 'I know nothing about football, and this lot'–waving an arm in the general direction of the rest of the members of the board 'know a bloody sight less'.

Well, I thought to myself, that can't be a bad introduction to life 'on the other side'.

But it didn't take me long to know I had found a grand place to start learning a completely new trade. Believe me, if players think their life is fraught, they should try being a manager!

Yet but for a twist of fate I might have gone somewhere entirely different from the Arsenal ground where I spent nine years as a player. It involved Jimmy Adamson, who was then playing for Burnley. The way it happened was like this.

Roy Peskett, a well-known Fleet Street football writer and an old friend of mine, had heard down the grapevine–as these chaps do–that Joe Mears was looking for a coach to help Ted Drake at Stamford Bridge.

It was February, 1961 and Roy asked Walter Winterbottom,

who was then head of the FA's coaching system, who was the best young coach in the country. Walter answered: 'There are two—Jimmy Adamson and Tommy Docherty.' Because Jimmy wanted to continue playing for a little while longer, Roy thought I'd stand a good chance if I applied. And he sat down and helped me write out my letter of application!

I went along to the Bridge wondering how I would fare, but I was put at my ease by Ted Drake. He explained that he and Vic Buckingham were friends from the old days in the war when they were in the Forces together, and he rated him highly as a coach, but that didn't mean anything personal as far as I was concerned.

'That's all right by me, Mr Drake,' I replied and after that we always got on well together. Later I was to succeed him.

I was interviewed by Mr Mears and his board and it was my first inkling of how strong a man he was. They asked me questions about my playing career, what I wanted out of life and so on. He asked me what my hobbies were and I replied 'Football'. It wasn't said to impress—it was just the truth.

My salary would be about £30 a week—if I got the job. He said he had other people to interview, but I understand that he only saw one, and I never knew his identity. A few days later I was told 'The job's yours'.

That was the start of a terrific relationship between myself and Mr Mears which blossomed much more when I later became manager. He was a man who didn't say a lot, but when he had something to say he'd tell you straight. He never minced words. I always appreciated the way he operated, and he certainly wasn't in any way a publicity-seeker like so many chairmen are today.

After I had been there a year or two, incidentally, I thought to myself: if anything ever happens to Joe Mears, I'll leave. That's the way it turned out eventually.

But there was I starting out on the road to be a manager, but without having quite finished as a player, as it happened. For though the rest of that 1960-61 season was spent in coaching duties, a tour of Israel and so on, the beginning of the next season saw problems arising on the field which culminated in the veteran Docherty making a playing 'come-back'.

Before that happened, I had a close-hand look at one of football's all-time greats, Jimmy Greaves. The sad part about it was that almost as soon as I arrived at Chelsea, the deal with AC Milan was arranged which would take Jimmy to the land of the lire.

If he had stayed at Chelsea, we would have won the League championship half-a-dozen times—of that I have no doubt. He was out of this world when it came to finishing.

At that precise time, the battle was well and truly on between the players, led by Jimmy Hill, and the Football League over the lifting of the maximum wage.

Jimmy Greaves' sole idea of going to Italy was to earn something like a wage in line with his tremendous talents.

The irony was that had he stayed at Chelsea for a few more months, they would have been able to match Milan's offer because by that time the maximum wage had been abolished, and the way was open for clubs to pay players what they wanted for the first time.

At the back end of my first season with Chelsea, our form was in and out and we finished just below half-way. But during that period Jimmy showed his magic at St James's Park where we gained a new club away record by winning 6-1 against Newcastle, with Greavesy grabbing four of them.

Also at this time, Chelsea's youth team included such names as Peter Bonetti, Bobby Tambling, Barry Bridges, Bert Murray, Terry Venables, and Ron and Allan Harris. That was one of the reasons why I was glad to be at Stamford Bridge—I could see in these young players the basis of a formidable team in the years ahead. The potential was almost frightening.

When eventually Jimmy Greaves was ready to come back to English football, I felt Chelsea made a cardinal error in sending the secretary John Battersby to Italy in an attempt to persuade him to come back to the Bridge. They should have sent me instead.

This in no way is meant to detract from John's efforts. He would only have been able to talk money to Jimmy whereas I could have chatted to him player to player with the different aspects that would have entailed.

In the end, Spurs made a more attractive offer and Chelsea lost Jimmy for good, which was a shame for he was an exceptional player and what Chelsea would have achieved with him alongside all the other talents still leaves me breathless when I think about it.

Trying to replace Jimmy in the side for the 1961-62 season was virtually impossible. Ted had his problems from the outset and although Bobby Tambling got among the goals immediately, we won only two out of the first six games.

It was at that point that he decided that I should put my playing experience to good use by appearing in the first team. Curiously enough, Terry Venables, who was then only 19 and had brilliant potential, made way for my inclusion in the side.

We won our first match 6-1 against Sheffield United (strange to think they're now in the Fourth Division) and Tambling hit three. But we couldn't sustain it and I had made only four appearances when the board acted.

Ted and I were on the point of travelling up to Scotland to have a look at Pat Crerand and Dave Mackay. We had made our plans to fly up in the afternoon for an evening match and I was waiting in Ted's office when the secretary came in and announced 'Mr Drake's got the sack. The board would like to see you.'

My mind was in a whirl. 'Mr Drake's leaving the club and we would like you to look after things as caretaker until such time as a new manager is appointed,' they told me. They knew I was about to leave for Glasgow and said 'If you want to go ahead, do so.'

I declined saying that I felt it was a pointless exercise, because I knew exactly what the players were capable of, and in any case, they just weren't available, so it would be a wasted journey anyway.

So I carried on until Christmas, but it was tough. By that time we were bottom of the First Division. Mr Mears had been away ill and there was I thinking that if this is what managerial life was all about, someone should have told me!

But as soon as Mr Mears was back in January, they had a board meeting which resulted in them offering me the manager's post. They'd said I'd done enough to prove I could do a job for them, which considering our plight, I thought was terrific.

I mused to myself: if they are offering me the job for three years at £3,000 a year while we're on the bottom of the table, they must have some regard for me.

I knew at that stage it would take a miracle to save us from relegation, and I was a bit short on miracles at the time. It was the story I was to find uncannily familiar as the years went by—inheriting a team which was getting old, with some players dodging about the club and not particularly interested in whether we stayed up or down.

We had some marvellous young players about to come good, but they didn't yet have enough know-how to save us—and down we went.

With that youth scheme though—a marvellous one which existed at the time under Dick Foss, with Jimmy Thompson, the chief scout, unearthing schoolboy players with extraordinary foresight and carving a record second to none for finding talent—the horizon wasn't so black.

It was Thompson who found the Greaveses, the Venables, the Harrises, the Tamblings and the Bridges. Yet some time later I found I had to dispense with his services and I took a lot of flak for that. I made no apologies for it at the time—and all these years afterwards I stand by what I did.

I formed the opinion that we weren't getting one hundred per cent of Jimmy's efforts, although he was our full-time chief scout and had been for a number of years.

Jimmy did a marvellous job for Chelsea up to the time they introduced stricter rules for the signing of schoolboys. Once the restrictions came into force, including limitations on how the approach to youngsters should be made, Jimmy was totally lost.

It was I who told the players of my appointment as manager, saying to them, tongue-in-cheek, 'From now on, you call me Mr Docherty.' This was greeted with hoots, ironic cheers and a few cracks, because they already knew me well enough to call me 'Boss'.

Whatever I wanted to be called, it made not a scrap of difference to the results, and we got deeper and deeper into trouble.

I had to search around for fresh players, there was no other way. So up I went to take a look at two Arbroath players in a match against East Stirling. But my eye immediately fell on a young full-back playing for East Stirling and I realised here was a gem buried in the lower divisions of Scottish soccer. His name was Eddie McCreadie.

Trying not to look too concerned after the game, I approached the East Stirling manager and asked him, in as casual a way as I could, how much he'd take for him. He seemed to be as cautious as me. Tentatively he replied 'Say £5,000?' 'Done,' I said, getting permission to speak to the player. It was one of my best-ever signings. In fact later, when the young side began to settle and get to know each other, I reckoned I had the best pair of full-backs anywhere – Ken Shellito and McCreadie.

Shellito was the best right back I have ever seen, and I've seen a few. If he hadn't had his career cut short by a knee injury, he'd have picked up lots more England international caps than his solitary one against Czechoslovakia.

Anyway, we were in the Second Division whether we liked it or not, but we were determined it would be only a short stay – and so it was.

We had one thing going for us – three terrific, experienced pros around which I was able to blend the kids who included Bonetti, one of the greatest of post-war English goalkeepers.

The trio were Frank Blunstone, a tricky outside left who won England honours and who later in my career teamed up with me at Derby; John Mortimore, a dependable, highly professional centre-half who is now assistant to Lawrie McMenemy at Southampton; and Frank Upton, who was not what one would call a great player, but a wise, thorough and reliable performer who always gave a hundred per cent. With them was this crowd of amazing teenagers, with Tambling, then only 20, as the skipper.

At one time we threatened to run away with the Second Division—in fact if I recollect, we were eight points in front at Christmas. But it was the year of the dreaded freeze-up when winter's grip froze everything solid—including soccer—until early March.

When we emerged from it, and started playing again, I began to wish the snow would tumble down again, for we lost four games in a row and soon that big lead was whittled down to next to nothing.

It called for decisive action. I telephoned Mr Mears, who was having a break in the south of France and asked him to make available £45,000 for Derek Kevan, the big, blond West Bromwich Albion striker.

'We shall have to start scoring goals, or we shall miss the boat,' I warned him.

It was a mistake. Derek took one look at the rigorous training methods which I insisted upon at Stamford Bridge, and wobbled at the knees at the mere thought of it. He'd not been used to that.

Ron Harris being chosen as captain of the England team which won the international youth tournament was about the only bright spot in a bleak spell, if you don't count three of our young players being picked for the England Under 23s.

Everything was building up to a situation we would rather not have faced. Our fixture at Sunderland, one of our promotion rivals, which was postponed from the snowy period in mid-January, loomed up suddenly as a crunch game.

Stoke were the other team involved and what it meant was that Sunderland needed only a point to go up, while we needed both and then had also to win at home to Portsmouth three days later to make sure.

Imagine the effect on the nerve-ends when we sat in our hotel on Wearside the night before the game and contemplated the top of the table looking like this:

|  | P | W | D | L | Goals | Pts | Goal average |
|---|---|---|---|---|---|---|---|
| Sunderland | 41 | 20 | 12 | 9 | 84-54 | 52 | 1.55 |
| Stoke City | 40 | 19 | 13 | 8 | 71-48 | 51 | 1.47 |
| Chelsea | 40 | 22 | 4 | 14 | 73-42 | 48 | 1.74 |

It was, without exaggeration, one of the most important games in my whole career, not only up to then, but since. It's a match the older Chelsea fans still talk about, for many of them made the tiring journey north to roar us on—and how we needed it at Roker which is a hotbed of partisanship at the best of times.

I ran over and over in my mind what team to play and decided, like a man playing cards for high stakes, to gamble. I dropped Bridges, Murray and Moore, played Kevan and Upton, switched Blunstone to the right wing and restored Tambling. That last move proved the decisive factor.

Also I drafted in little Tommy Harmer, one of the smallest men ever to play top-class football, for only his fifth senior game of the season. It was no occasion for the purists and we went at it hard, trying to unsettle Sunderland. It wasn't pretty but it worked.

Just before half-time came our vital chance. Tambling's corner came to Tommy Harmer and somehow he bundled it in with his stomach, thereafter telling his mates in the dressing-room they would have to re-name him 'Tummy' Harmer.

The second half put years on me. In the fourth minute of injury time George Mullhall, the Scots winger, beat Ken Shellito for the first time in the match and unleashed a thunderbolt. A goal would have put Sunderland up, but Bonetti somehow deflected the ball away and it was all over.

We were over the worst hurdle and really our boys were in no mood to miss going up now. We slaughtered poor Pompey 7-0 on the Tuesday. Tambling hit four himself and we went up on goal average, with Sunderland the unlucky ones. Ironically, Kevan headed a goal which started the romp—the only one he scored for us in seven games before I sold him to Manchester City.

Derek could never take the strenuous demands I put upon my players. Harry Medhurst summed it up after we won promotion, saying: 'When Tommy first came, he was unpopular because of the iron discipline he imposed at the club. Now we would follow him anywhere—he's won our respect.'

Curiously enough, Harry was by my side when I had to apply that discipline in the notorious Blackpool incident, of which more later.

Having won our place back in the First Division, and being described by the writers as one of the finest young teams in the land, we enjoyed a spell of stability and partial success for the next three or four years.

In our first season back we finished fifth, only seven points behind the champions Liverpool. We then ended up third (five points off the Championship), fifth and ninth, and in three successive seasons won a place in the semi-finals of the FA Cup.

Of course, all good things never last and there were one or two clouds beginning to blot my horizon. Soon I was to face the sort of tests which come to most managers once in a while, but which seem to have dogged me, although I never went looking for them.

I found I was later accused of breaking up the successful Chelsea side. That was untrue. The team broke itself up.

My managerial policy has always been to seek a better player than the one I have got in each position. You must never be satisfied with what you've got—if you are, then in my book you're in trouble.

Some of my players began to get a bit greedy. Human nature, I suppose, but a problem for any manager. Then came the Blackpool business. All these factors contributed to what was called the break-up of the Chelsea team.

It wasn't a sudden business, by any means. In the meantime we were shaking a few famous clubs.

We won the League Cup in 1964-65 against Leicester, which put us into the Fairs Cup the following season, and we seemed to be involved in everything at that stage. In under a month we had accounted for Liverpool and Leeds in the FA Cup (and that entailed beating Bill Shankly's men at Anfield!) and AC Milan in the Fairs Cup, after three terrific games, culminating in a play-off in Italy in which we got through on the away goals rule, with a performance the chairman and myself rated the finest we ever saw Chelsea give.

But the cracks were beginning to appear and before another row loomed up in which the Spanish club Barcelona levelled a charge against me of cheating, matters came to a head between myself and Terry Venables.

For some reason, there has always been a form of antipathy between Terry and me which doesn't affect my regard for his ability as a player or later as a manager. We never got off on the right foot and when you consider I had to get him out of Chelsea when he was the tender age of 21 because I felt there could be only one boss on the playing side, you can appreciate the depth of the personality clash.

I had been mulling it over in my mind for some 12 months before I took the step which I knew would be highly controversial as soon as it was revealed.

It was February, 1966. I put Terry on the transfer list and made it absolutely plain that there was no future for him at Stamford Bridge.

He was a thorn in my side. In training he would always be questioning my tactics or decisions, and it seemed to me trying to demean me in front of the other players. He was a confident chappie who was just too damned cheeky for my well-being.

What the other players didn't know was that he often came to my office quietly without anyone else around, and apologised for causing trouble. If the others had known this, his standing in their eyes might not have been so grand.

When at last the crunch came and I told him he was on the list, he looked genuinely shocked. I told him in my view he had been playing for himself and not the team. Of course, I might have known – I was slammed in the Press, which was hardly surprising because Terry had a lot of friends in Fleet Street. But they weren't at the training sessions when he was taking the mickey and undermining my authority.

Terry took it badly. He got married and I was the only person on the Chelsea staff – playing or admin – who didn't at first receive an invitation to the wedding. His last game for Chelsea was against Barcelona in the Fairs Cup and he then joined Spurs.

The Barcelona involvement caused a rumpus. The first leg tie was scheduled at a time when we had one of the wettest spells I can ever remember and the Bridge pitch slowly turned into a quagmire. Against my wishes, the Spaniards trained on the pitch the night previously during the rain and cut it up so much that our groundsman couldn't get at it to repair the damage – and in the meantime the rain increased in intensity.

We had a crop of injuries at the time and an FA Cup semi-final looming up on the following Saturday against Sheffield Wednesday at Villa Park. Barcelona knew this and to my astonishment, though the Swedish referee took one look at the pitch and said there would be no match, the Spaniards flew off the handle.

They accused me of influencing the ref because of the seriousness of my injury list, and then really flipped their lid, suggesting that I had deliberately watered the pitch to make it unplayable.

Anyone around who had witnessed the amount of rainfall which had fallen could see that was preposterous. We had, in the end, to ask Sir Stanley Rous to explain to the angry Spaniards that it was the referee's decision not to play the game, and his alone.

Personally, I wished the game had gone on – I reckon we'd have done them good and proper, even with our injuries. As fate had it, the tie went to three matches, the last being a play-off which the Spaniards won 5-0 in Barcelona.

In the middle of it all, I actually tendered my resignation when I learned that two of my best players, Bonetti and Tambling, had not only refused new and splendid terms offered by the club, but had gone one step further and had asked for a move.

We had done so well that season without actually winning anything, that the board were shocked. Money was at the root of it all, naturally. But I discovered that part of the problem was that they thought they were spending too much time away from home. Their wives were complaining, which must have also inflamed the situation.

Peter's wife said to me: 'They're always away – they're never at home.' My reply was: 'Listen, Frances, in football, when you're successful, you're always away – making money. But if you're not happy with Peter being away from home, we'll get him a job as a postman.' Ironically, I believe that is the job he is doing today!

I added: 'You don't see the Orient players going away – because they never win anything.'

Even John Battersby, who was a good secretary, used to moan

about all the all-ticket matches he had to contend with at the Bridge.

I said to him once: 'If you don't like it here, go to Orient or Brentford as secretary—they never have any ticket problems there!'

Well, this upset with Peter and Bobby came to a head when the chairman asked me if it was necessary to take the players away so often. I replied that our travelling and our success went hand-in-hand, and had made a pile of money for the club and the players, who were among the highest-paid in the game. They had no cause to grumble.

I added that if the board agreed to the two players' demands, I couldn't stay on as manager.

He refused to accept my offer of resignation, and after looking at me for a few moments, remarked 'You must do the job as you see it. I shouldn't have interfered, but I honestly thought I was doing the best for the club.'

In a fortnight, both players had withdrawn their requests. And later, at a Supporters Club dinner, Mr Mears told the players point-blank that they were professionals and at the top for such a relatively short space of time, that they must be dedicated to success, even though it meant a longer amount of time they were on duty for the club. I had made my point.

But Mr Mears' health was already beginning to fail, and with it, my time at Chelsea was drawing nearer to its end.

I had another season to run. Little did I know then that it would be the longest spell as a manager that I would enjoy with one club...

# 14
# The Famous Blackpool Incident

THERE COMES a time in every man's career when he faces the supreme test of his judgment and his character – when he tackles a difficult decision and decides to go one way, whatever the consequences.

The first time I came up against a situation like that as a manager was in 1965 when I had been in charge at Chelsea for just over three years.

The outcome involved me and the club in some of the most sensational headlines and stories ever written about the game. Even today, 16 years later, when you mention 'the Blackpool incident', older fans will immediately know to what you are referring.

It was the day I sent eight senior Chelsea players home from a seaside break for a grave breach of club discipline. When the news broke and its full implication was realised, it hit the game like a bombshell.

As the man who ordered my players home, I was both praised and criticised. Yet faced with the same circumstances I would do precisely the same thing again, even though the mere thought of it later moved me to tears.

It was the hardest – yet in some ways – boldest decision I ever made. And until this time, I have refrained from telling my detailed side of the story because I felt it would have harmed the playing careers of the men involved as well as putting them under some domestic strain.

So this is the Doc's-eye view of the famous Blackpool incident the like of which soccer has never seen before–or, happily, since.

A break by the sea at Blackpool was something we had introduced when travelling north for matches. It began to be very popular–the players loved it, it did them good and it was money well spent. It also broke up the humdrum of training in midweek at home.

During the evenings, I permitted the players to go out for a drink as long as they were in by between eleven and twelve o'clock, preferably nearer eleven than midnight. For a while there were no problems.

Towards the end of the 1964-65 season we had cause for being very satisfied with ourselves. We were pushing for the League championship. We had reached the semi-final of the FA Cup only to lose 2-0 to Liverpool, and we had won the League Cup in a two-leg final with Leicester City, which guaranteed us a place in Europe for the following season.

So with two games left, it was an ideal time to go again to Blackpool for a breather before we summoned ourselves for a last big effort.

On the night in question, I had told the players to be in by about 10.30 pm. Some of them were a bit late, running in puffing and panting, and the last in was John Hollins, a super pro.

'Do you want some tea,' I asked them. 'No thanks boss,' they said. 'We've had something.'

That evening I was sitting quietly with Harry Medhurst our trainer, Dr Bowen the club doctor, and Ron Suart, who was at the time manager of Blackpool.

Ron even remarked to me–and looking back, there was a touch of irony about this–'Isn't it marvellous, the way you've got them together,' he said. 'If you keep it up, there's no knowing what you'll achieve.'

'Yes,' I replied, 'they're a super set of lads.' And I meant it–they were. What I didn't know was that they were about to let me, and themselves, down, with a bang.

Over an hour later, about midnight, the hotel porter came up and said to me quietly: 'Mr Docherty—your boys have caused a terrible rumpus upstairs.'

My reaction was one of immediate disbelief. 'Not my boys – they know better. They're not like that,' I replied with conviction. I knew that a rugger team were also staying at the hotel, and I was convinced that if there had been any trouble, it would have been them—not my players. And I told the porter so.

He went away but he was back soon. 'They're still at it,' he asserted, 'and what's more the door to the fire escape is open.'

What I didn't know at the time was that when someone goes out through the fire escape for reasons other than a fire, he breaks the hotel rules, because the hotel then becomes liable if anyone comes through and steals anything.

'Get the key,' I told the porter, intending to prove to him once and for all that my players were safely in their rooms where they should be. Imagine my shock when we examined four or five of the rooms and found them all empty. We went downstairs again to await developments. I couldn't do much else at the time.

It wasn't until about 3.30 am that the porter returned. 'They've come in now,' he said.

Up I went again, this time to find several pairs of blinking eyes peering at me as I opened the hotel rooms one by one, as if they had just been awakened by my entrance.

When I look back now after all these years, I have to smile at the incongruous nature of it all. But that night it wasn't funny. I was fuming.

In one of the rooms, there was a situation like a Brian Rix farce. Johnny Hollins was sharing the room with his great pal Barry Bridges. They were both terrific fellows and good professionals.

'All right, lads, sleeping okay?' I enquired, trying to hide the sarcasm in my voice. 'Yes, boss,' they croaked. I stepped forward armed with the knowledge that the rooms had been empty not long before and pulled back the sheets.

They were both lying there with their suits, collars and ties on, looking as though they had just come in and were ready to go out again. To this day I don't know how I kept a straight face, thinking it was something I might have done myself when I was younger.

Anyway, I was the boss, and I knew I had a serious matter on my hands and that if I faltered, I would never again be able to command any respect or discipline.

I told them both to report to me in the morning for their rail tickets, because I would be sending them home.

And I told the others the same, eight in all. 'I've got to make a stand right now,' I said. 'It's gone far enough—it's either you or me.' As well as Hollins and Bridges, the group included Eddie McCreadie and Terry Venables.

I might have known I'd have most trouble with Venables. He was always the ringleader, the 'King of the Kids', a good player among the youngsters, in charge of them so to speak, the 'gang leader'. They followed him and looked up to him, and he knew it. He wasn't even in his room when I checked again. So I went back later, and this time he was there. 'You've been out—where have you been?' I asked.

He denied it and said he had been in McCreadie's room all evening. I knew that was a lie because I had checked Eddie's room and found it empty. When I told Venables this he persisted. I was getting angry.

I told Terry I had been good to them, allowed them out during the evenings, and that basically we were in Blackpool to prepare for important matches, not skylark about. I told him everyone else had admitted going out, except him. Even then he wouldn't change his story.

The next morning they all went back to London on the train, leaving me with only eight players in Blackpool.

It was inevitable that the story would leak out, but because the hotel porter tipped off the local Press, it was out sooner than I expected.

All hell broke loose. The Press had a field day. Some took the view that I had been brave and had done the right thing. Others said I should have thought it over, and was again being impulsive.

But what they didn't know was that I *had* thought about it—before it happened. Many times before, I had conjured up in

The girl who cost me my job—but I have no regrets.
Mary and I with our daughter Grace (*Author's picture*)

*Above:* Willie Morgan playing for
Manchester United. It was
remarks made by Willie in a
television programme which
eventually led to my two well
publicised court cases (*Colorsport*)

*Right:* Denis Law, a great player
who was not happy with me over
the way he left United (*Colorsport*)

*Top:* Paddy Crerand, my assistant at Manchester United, and I watch a match in the 1973-74 season. In 1976 we nearly came to blows after the Cup Final (*Colorsport*)

*Above:* The Cup success of 1977. Tommy Cavanagh, myself, Frank Blunstone and Laurie Brown preparing to drink to the victory (*Manchester Evening News*)

*Right:* A lovely, big, warm and hospitable man. I was angry and sad at the death of United chairman Louis Edwards (*Sporting Pictures (UK) Ltd*)

*Above:* Sir Matt Busby with the European Cup. We all loved Matt, but I think he should have been less lovable and more strict (*Colorsport*)

*Right:* George Best—a genius whose career might have been longer with an earlier marriage or firmer discipline from the club (*Colorsport*)

*Above:* Jim Gregory owns and runs Queen's Park Rangers. In our dealings he leads me by two sackings to one walk-out (*Sporting Pictures (UK) Ltd*)

*Right:* Bobby Charlton. In my view Bobby would have made a great United manager (*Colorsport*)

*Opposite left:* You can see the class
... The youngish Tommy
Docherty in his Arsenal days
(*Colorsport*)

*Above left:* Brian Clough–too good
at his job for the FA to ask him to
be England manager. He would
tread on a few toes (*Colorsport*)

*Above right:* Managers today have
a far more difficult job than their
predecessors. The most successful
in Britain is Bob Paisley, my No. 1
(*Colorsport*)

*Right:* Jimmy Hill has been good
for the game, and I would like to
see him become chairman of the
Football Association (*Sporting
Pictures (UK) Ltd*)

*Above left:* Frank O'Farrell, an old
friend. I was told that he would be
sacked at Manchester United and
the job would be mine (*Colorsport*)

*Above right:* My successor at
United, Dave Sexton, a quiet man
who failed to inspire the team and
was sacked in 1981 (*Colorsport*)

*Left:* Bruce Rioch. I fined him as a
player. How will he fare as a
manager? (*Author's picture*)

*Opposite top:* Bill Nicholson and I
with the FA Cup at a reception in
the Hilton Hotel after the 1967
Final. I had some unscheduled
words to say about one or two
grievances (*Associated Newspapers
Ltd*)

*Opposite below:* Disappointment
again in 1976. I look thoroughly
fed up at the Cup Final defeat by
outsiders Southampton (*Press
Association*)

*Above left:* Willie Ormond took over from me as Scotland's team manager. I think he should have got about more (*Colorsport*)

*Above right:* I had to transfer Terry Venables from Chelsea. I had the feeling he was taking the mickey (*Sporting Pictures (UK) Ltd*)

*Left:* If we had to lose the Cup Final of 1976, then we couldn't have lost to nicer guys than Lawrie McMenemy and his men (*Sporting Pictures (UK) Ltd*)

Clive Thomas indicating he'd
blown for time as Zico was
'scoring' for Brazil in a World
Cup match in 1978. All in the
day's work for controversial Clive
(*Colorsport*)

*Above:* Derek Henderson, who helped me with this book, and I at one of our meetings at Deepdale (*Hamlyn Group Picture Library*)

*Below:* Now for the future . . . With the Preston North End players before the start of the 1981-82 season (*Sporting Pictures (UK) Ltd*)

my mind situations just like the Blackpool incident, asking myself 'If that sort of thing happened to me, what would I do? How would I react?'

What caused most of the furore afterwards was Venables' talking to newspapermen and declaring that the players had not done what was being suggested – but the fact was that no one had suggested what they *were* doing!

He inflamed it by saying 'We went out for a few drinks and picked up a couple of girls.' But the father of one of the girls took offence at the phrase 'picked up', saying it implied his daughter's morals were in question.

The father came to me and I had to sort it out. I told him no real harm had been done, the players were young and if he left it with me, I would be taking action in the shape of heavy fines. So talk of Chelsea being sued evaporated, the parents were very nice about the whole thing, and matters took their course.

The board's attitude meant a lot to me at the time. Joe Mears was abroad and clearly wasn't well versed on what had actually happened at Blackpool. I had a telegram from him saying 'Don't know the situation as it stands – but we back your decision 110 per cent,' which was fantastic.

Clubs from overseas wrote to me and congratulated me on my action. Bob Lord wrote an article in a newspaper declaring that 'if there were more managers like Tommy Docherty, football would be in a much better shape'.

It was a source of both amusement and irony to me a couple of years later when there were other incidents in soccer involving decisions by managers to impose discipline on their players after mishaps. Then newspapers which had criticised me at the time of the Blackpool incident, changed their tune and said 'In retrospect, what Tommy Docherty did was absolutely right.'

What happened as a direct result of my decision is a matter of soccer history. None of those eight played in the first team at Burnley on the following Saturday, and not surprisingly we lost 6-2.

So you could say I threw away what chance we had of winning the League championship on a matter of principle.

# 15
# The Rome Rough-house and Happier Trips

IN ITALY the word soccer is a misnomer. They should substitute the word thuggery and that would be far more appropriate.

In short, Italian football is a disgrace. It has been for many years, and nothing I have seen or heard convinces me that anything is about to change. It is a great pity because so many Italian players are extremely talented.

It is foolish to excuse their shameful, snide way of playing by saying it is down to the Latin temperament. Players like Pelé, Gerson and Didi never had to resort to vicious tactics to win matches.

The Latin temperament for the Italians has been a licence to spit, elbow, dig, kick and gouge their way through a multitude of matches at both club and international level for many years now, and I'm amazed that officialdom has not taken a harder line.

The Scots and the Welsh are said to be fiery—and so they are—but this does not mean they go about kicking players indiscriminately and using national fervour on the soccer field as an excuse for it.

Even in Australia—and you may find this hard to believe so many thousands of miles away from Italy—the behaviour of Italian teams is nothing short of assault and battery at times. It seems built into the Italian nature, just as it has been at times with the Argentinians and the Uruguayans—but fortunately those two countries have gradually learned to keep it under wraps.

I will never forget our experience with Juventus of Turin while I was United manager. It was 1976-77 and the UEFA Cup second round brought us together, with the first leg at Old Trafford.

We won 1-0 with a goal from Gordon Hill. There was plenty of evidence of thuggery from them in that first leg which should have given us a fair idea of what to expect in the return leg.

What we certainly didn't expect happened actually in the tunnel when the two teams were lining up side by side waiting to come out for the game. Despite the presence of the Hungarian referee, the Juventus players just stood there and spat at my players—without any provocation whatsoever!

The sad thing was that they were such a talented team—with about eight men in the international side at the time—that they didn't need to stoop to this to unnerve us.

Out on the pitch there was worse to come. Over-the-ball tackling, poking in the eyes, pulling us up by the armpits after they had felled us and squeezing their fingers to such an extent that it really hurt—they did it all.

They also won 3-0 to go through on aggregate and indeed they went on to win the final. That's not what we'll remember them for . . .

But my first real experience of what depths Italian teams—and also Italian spectators—can sink to came back in 1965 when I was Chelsea manager.

It was September and Chelsea's first taste of European competition. We had been drawn at home in the first leg of what was then called the Inter-Cities Fairs Cup to AS Roma. It was a first round match and we had prepared ourselves seriously. The weekend beforehand, I took my coach Jimmy Andrews and my skipper Terry Venables with me to watch our opponents in action.

What we saw made us realise we were in for a couple of none-too-easy ties, but that was all. We little dreamed that it would lead to practically an international incident.

As it turned out, I was about to experience the roughest, nastiest and most disgraceful exhibition of all that is worst in football—and certainly the most shameful it has even been my misfortune to be involved in during a career in soccer spanning 35 years.

We had qualified for the Fairs Cup by winning the Football

League Cup the previous season against Leicester on a 3-2 aggregate, and with European competition beginning really to catch the public's imagination, we were very pleased to be in it.

What happened when we visited Rome was a direct result of what occurred in the first leg at Stamford Bridge, and also a venomous campaign of hate built up in the Italian Press which set the explosive scene for our visit.

From our point of view, the only reprehensible thing about the first leg was the attitude of the Chelsea crowd towards Roma and the fact that their team coach had to undergo a bit of bumping and banging from a few angry fans as they left our ground.

But while I deplored that, what they had seen on the field from the Roma players had incited them. While I did not condone it, I could fully understand it.

For after a flashpoint during which Eddie McCreadie was sent off, my players had to run the gauntlet of what one paper described at the time as 'punching, butting and wild senseless kicking'—and they weren't referring to an assault on the ball, either!

Poor Eddie lost his head momentarily in a retaliatory foul on the Italian player Leonardi, who had kicked him violently on the shin causing a great gash in his leg. After he had shoulder-charged the Italians' No. 2, Eddie was grabbed around the throat by Leonardi. He hit out—and that was marching orders for him after less than half an hour.

Considering our plight in being down to 10 men, we managed a magnificent result, winning 4-1 with Venables scoring a brilliant hat-trick. Even when Terry was viciously kicked under the referee's nose and was carried to the dressing-room, there was no disciplinary action at all for the offending Roma player.

So the stage was set for Rome—and throwing the Christians to the lions wasn't in it.

We guessed there might be a little repercussion because of the roughness of the first tie, and I was aware that the Press had built up something of a hate campaign against us, but I didn't imagine its strength or that the outcome would be as dramatic.

The stories they had been telling their readers were straight out of a horror comic. One was that when the Italian chairman had come into our dressing room at Stamford Bridge after the first tie to congratulate my players, he was spat at and thrown out!

The McCreadie incident, of course, was given the full treatment with the exception that what Leonardi had perpetrated had been conveniently ignored. We were labelled 'killers' and the atmosphere was decidedly icy when we landed in Rome 24 hours before the match, although the actual temperature was high, it being September.

If we expected a party of officials from Roma to greet us, we were disappointed. There wasn't a soul at the airport from the host club. Also nobody from Roma at the hotel, no messages...

We had been under the impression that the game was to be held in the national stadium which holds 100,000 people. Instead it was switched to Tibitsi Roma, a very pleasant but much smaller ground belonging to a Third Division club, built something like a bull-ring.

I smiled to myself later that this was somewhat appropriate in the circumstances ... It was certainly ideal for what the Italians had their minds set on.

The air was hostile, but that was nothing unusual and we took little notice—until the game started, that is.

During the preliminaries, the Italian police had been conspicuous by their absence—almost as if they'd been kept away. What few there were made absolutely no attempt to intervene when we stepped off the coach to meet shaking fists and oaths of all descriptions, none of which we understood. But we could read the signs.

When Joe Mears, our chairman, his son David and some of the directors walked on to the pitch to have a look at it, the first of the missiles began to rain down. One tomato thudded against David Mears' suit.

And when, without any escort or guidance, the party went to look for their seats, they had to shoulder their way through jeering, hostile fans to seats which had been reserved—not in the VIP's box where you would expect guests to be, but some way away.

This was in total contrast to the way we had looked after Roma officials in London and how we always treated our guests – courteously.

Once the Chelsea team came into full view past the fencing around the players' tunnel, the missiles increased in intensity.

By the time the kick-around had ended, Peter Bonetti's goalmouth was littered with all manner of rubbish – bottles, fruit, cans and so on. The ground staff made no attempt to clear the rubbish from the pitch and so we started with it remaining there.

I had been very pointed about self-discipline in my pre-match talk to the players. I had told them that whatever the Italians did, retaliation was strictly out. I said the Italians would be hell bent on provoking us into any sort of incident, but that if we responded in any way, it would be playing into their hands. And we weren't going to toss away that 4-1 advantage with foolish actions.

Though I hoped they would listen, I reckoned without their own bearing. They were all magnificent. What they went through was the greatest provocation I have ever seen a team face.

When I and my colleagues and the substitutes prepared to sit on the bench, one of the Roma officials said 'No – you're over there.' We soon found out why. We were placed in front of the terracing where most of the hooligan spectators were congregated.

Facing missiles was bad enough, but when we realised there were cups full of urine being hurled at us, the whole exhibition took on a more degrading turn. While the crowd felt there was a chance that all this intimidation might make us crack, they kept up their bombardment.

When Marvin Hinton was chopped down, the West German referee seemed about to send off the offending Roma player. But very wisely he had second thoughts as the Italian staggered away feigning injury, as Italians often do when they've committed a bad foul themselves.

The Italian team manager made efforts to try to curb the crowd's actions, without avail.

After half-time, our players achieved a cute dodge. Each one made sure he was close to one of his opponents as we came out for the second half. The Italian players spotted this and tried to 'get away' from us, realising that the missiles wouldn't zoom in on us alone!

It was almost comical to see them running away from our players who, at the same time, tried to stick close to them!

Then one of the worst incidents came when John Boyle was laid unconscious by a bottle which hit him as he was about to deliver a throw-in.

The hold-up lasted five minutes while the fans screamed for the game to be re-started and John to be bodily removed from the pitch. But he eventually recovered and there was an amusing incident in the middle of all the mayhem, when a tomato meant for one of us, hit an Italian player in the face. He reacted by shaking his fist at his own spectators.

It was ugly at times, particularly when an iron stanchion ripped from a seat thudded into the turf and stuck a couple of feet away from John Hollins. Then Eddie McCreadie was knocked out by a bottle.

This was more like war than football but as the game wore on, the crowd realised that our 4-1 lead was not going to be dented and we even heard some applause from the fairer spectators for some of our moves as we managed a goalless draw which saw us through comfortably.

But the end of the game was by no means the end of the hostilities. We spent an hour and a half in the dressing room hoping that the volatile fans would have long since dispersed. But no – they were waiting for their last piece of revenge.

There looked to be about a dozen police to control a mob of around 2,000 as we boarded our bus to go back to the hotel.

Objects started to smash into the side of the coach. The ladies in our party were told to crouch down on the floor and the players and others covered their faces with bags and cushions. No sooner had the luckless McCreadie done this than a lump of iron crashed through the window nearest him and thousands of pieces of glass cascaded all over the inside of the coach.

Sensibly the driver did not stop to ask questions. It took a while later to remove all the splinters from June Mears' hair as the chairman's daughter-in-law bravely smiled and looked relieved that at last it was all over.

The banquet, so-called, was gloomy. You could have sliced the atmosphere with a sword. The players kept apart and almost sullenly ate the meal. The Italian club's president apologised for the crowd's behaviour in a brief mention of the game but Mr Mears, replying, was dignified and straight to the point.

After all this time I can't remember the exact words, but he told them in no uncertain manner that Chelsea had undergone the greatest provocation any team had ever been asked to face and they had done it with pride and dignity.

We were glad to relax afterwards and stay up for a few quiet drinks. In the wee small hours, a small handful of the more embarrassed Italian journalists came to the hotel with the early morning papers and apologised to our club for the vitriol of their irresponsible colleagues – which was at least manly of them.

I gave them a few quotes which I said I hoped they would print. In effect, I said that if you rolled up everything nasty that had happened to me in my entire career, it wouldn't match the revolting nature of the Roma riot. Only one other English team I knew, West Ham, could have acted in such an exemplary way on a foreign field in such circumstances.

Nothing in the game, I told them as they scribbled away, had anything to do with civilised behaviour. The fans were animals and the only civilised people present were the Chelsea party. The way my players were kicked down from behind and got up and walked away was nothing short of magnificent. Our finest retaliation, I added, was to go through to the next round with a three-goal margin.

Back home, we received official recognition of our behaviour from the Minister of Sport, Denis Howell, himself a former League referee. 'Please convey to the club my congratulations on their conduct and composure which reflects great credit on British sport and upon themselves.'

Roma were banned for three years from European competition and deserved no less.

Perhaps the whole episode did have a little salutary effect, because although there was another disgraceful incident involving Lazio players during an Arsenal visit, with street violence outside a restaurant, we don't seem to have experienced anything quite so volatile since, though Italian on-the-field thuggery still rears its ugly head too often for my peace of mind.

A week later we were committed to returning to Italy for a game against a combined Milan team in connection with British Trades week. We were understandably a little apprehensive, but the game was uneventful, and trouble there was none.

We had seen at first hand the Mafia-type face of Italian soccer, and we didn't want to experience it ever again.

Happily, my other trips abroad with club sides have been predominantly delightful and tours I made in Haiti and Nigeria were full of extremely funny incidents which show the other side of soccer.

I've been on a lot of tours in my time and experienced some strange happenings. But those which took place in Haiti and Nigeria several years apart, are two of the weirdest which spring to mind.

The incident in the Central American republic of Haiti was really bizarre in many ways, and gave me my first insight into the voodoo I had read about but never come across in person.

It was at the tail-end of that trouble-marked tour of Bermuda and the other West Indian Islands which eventually culminated in my leaving Chelsea in 1967.

Once there I became very friendly with Antoine Tassey, the coach to the Haiti national team who got to the World Cup finals. He was a very talented coach and had done a good job with his players who showed us a high standard of skill.

The place was then run by the notorious 'Papa Doc' Duvalier— a much more powerful Doc than I! At dinner one night we had a little taste of the voodoo, with a chicken running about after its head had been cut off—not a pretty sight!

But one of the most amusing incidents concerned a reception after we had checked in at a hotel which had only been finished just prior to our arrival.

It was a nice place, with a new swimming pool that had never been used, good food and comfortable. But at night we could hear the steady drums beating in the distance and it reminded me of scenes from old movies I had seen about Central America.

We trained during the afternoon, and at night we stayed in our hotel–something we were advised to do–because it was a dictatorship and there were revolutionaries around all the time.

Anyway, the reception at the Town Hall was during a curious mixture of weather–sunshine and heavy showers. We all stood there with glasses of champagne in our hands. But the roof was leaky and the drops of rain either splashed straight into the champagne or splattered on top of our heads. But nobody batted an eyelid! It was altogether an extraordinary experience, and as much as we could do to control our amusement.

Even that didn't match the trip I made with QPR to Nigeria a couple of years ago. We found a country where corruption seemed to be the byword and where they don't put the same value on human life that we do.

We found that you had to pay to get into the country, and pay even more to get out–and everyone was on the make. Some of the situations were serious one moment, and absolutely hilarious the next.

I found out the hard way how to get a telephone call through to England after several unsuccessful attempts over a period or two or three days after we arrived. I particularly wanted to speak to Mary who was expecting our little girl at the time, and I was beginning to despair of getting a call through when I discovered that my youth team coach John Collins seemed to be managing it without undue trouble.

'What's the secret?' I asked him. 'Why don't you try giving the hotel telephonist a tip,' he replied. 'I tried to get through for two days without success, but when I handed him a fiver I got a call inside 10 minutes.'

I put it to the test. Once again I tried the conventional way–not a sausage. Next time the telephonist, whose name just had to be Tom, was more to the point. 'You must give me a tip,' he said, without any embarrassment at all. 'How much?' I asked. 'The same as Mr Collins gave me,' he replied. We agreed, and I put the phone down. Hardly had it rested on the receiver than it rang – and when I picked it up I heard Mary's voice.

Tom was on to a good thing. At least half a dozen times after that when I *hadn't* put a call through to the old country, the phone rang and Mary was on the other end – sometimes even two and three o'clock in the morning at my end.

Tom's voice kept on saying 'Hold on, Mr Doc – you're through to Mrs Brown' – and I hadn't booked any call. Obviously, Tom was a bit short of the readies and figured I was a handy benefactor.

So many things about the visit were good – the food, the hospitality, the hotel and the football, that it came as a shock to us to learn that they were getting bigger crowds at the big stadium for executions than for the soccer.

I was astonished to be told that the punishment for stealing from shops and suchlike was death, and that when the executions were staged in public, they charged spectators to go in and watch – and had tremendous attendances. Sometimes, it was as high as 30,000 – and the shooting was for real.

When the time came to leave, we discovered more about the corruption, this time around the vicinity of the airport. How they welcomed the sight of travellers!

If there was a plane with 400 seats about to leave, they'd issue 800 boarding passes and those who flashed the notes got on first.

In fact, you had to pay three times. Billy Hamilton had to leave the tour early to fly back to join Northern Ireland for the international championship and we gave him £30 for incidental expenses as he went to the airport.

It cost him £10 for his boarding pass even though his seat was already booked; £10 for passing through the check-in desk; and another £10 to get through customs. Talk about hush money!

When our plane actually soared into the air, you never heard such a roar of relief from the lads, although it had been an enjoyable trip and something remarkable to look back upon.

The tradesmen in Nigeria would barter for anything. They'd give you £50 worth of goods for your shoes. We tried to flog a set of QPR shirts to one street corner merchant but he wasn't having any, and shook his head. He was, he told us, a Manchester United supporter!

# 16
# Wembley – More Rows – and Fresh Pastures

I F J OE M EARS had not died of a heart attack, and instead had continued at the helm at Stamford Bridge, I would still be Chelsea's manager to this day.

That will sound presumptuous and almost silly in view of everything that has happened to me in the intervening years. But I base it on my magnificent relationship with Mr Mears and the way things started to slide for me once he had vacated the chair because of his failing health. At one time, I thought I was at Stamford Bridge for life, I was so happy there.

Once Mr Mears gave up the chairmanship, that was really the beginning of the end of my time there. From success and harmony, it steadily became a fraught situation, with me having a blazing row with the board over players' ticket allocations and bonuses, a public condemnation of me by the directors, and finally my suspension for a month by the FA after trouble on our tour of Bermuda.

You wouldn't think that in the midst of all this we had actually reached Wembley. But to complete the unhappy picture we lost the first all-London final to Tottenham. And 1967 was drawing to its close when I decided it was time to pack my bags and move on to fresh pastures.

All that furore earlier in the year gave me a real experience of some of the in-fighting and turmoil that was to become something of a hallmark in my career in later years and which helped to give me the reputation of being a controversial figure, when in reality all I ever wanted to do in any of my jobs was what was best for the club.

I suppose, looking back, that any chance I had of forging a good relationship with Charles Pratt, Joe Mears' successor as chairman, was blown when I told him: 'You've been 25 years as Joe's vice-chairman—and you've learned nothing.'

Mr Pratt was one of the old school. To him a cup was a cup. He wanted to know everything about the team, and to me that was intolerable. In my book a manager can't do his job while spending half his life keeping directors informed as to what he is doing. They pay him to manage—and he must manage.

I fell out with Mr Pratt once for a ridiculous reason. I hadn't told him what the Chelsea team would be for the five-a-side indoor tournament at Wembley. I thought it was crazy. Joe Mears never in his life—and I mean never—asked me what the team was.

In the end I chucked it in for a basic reason—I just didn't get on with Mr Pratt. And if you don't get on with your chairman, you've got to call it a day, because if you don't, every day seems longer . . .

In any event, the club had been through the trauma of two major rows under the public gaze even before the fuss over the Bermudan tour.

It all started when we reached the fourth round of the FA Cup and had to face Brighton, then a Third Division side.

In the dressing room before the kick-off of our home game with Manchester City, the players tackled me about the allocation of tickets for the tie at Brighton which was to be played a week later.

Without going into the exact details of what the players were allocated, what it boiled down to was that Mr Pratt and the secretary John Battersby declined to come and talk it over with the players.

I was in an invidious position. I feared that the players—four of whom lived either in Sussex or on the fringe of Brighton—might have supposed that I was the reason why they weren't getting as many tickets as they would have liked.

I was told in no uncertain terms by John Battersby that even if we got to Wembley, this was the sort of allocation the players could expect. The chairman didn't think there was any need for him or the secretary to justify their position to the players.

Now you may think all this was a bit trivial in the big scheme of things. But as a manager, it created added problems for me because I had the job of 'psyching' the players up for a difficult away Cup-tie hurdle at a time they were disgruntled over their tickets.

There is always an inference in the air when players want more tickets that they are after making a handsome profit in the ticket-tout business, and the Chelsea players resented it. In fact, apart from their usual complimentaries, they returned the other tickets to the club.

I vented my feelings in a newspaper article in which I said I felt so strongly about it that I forsook my own ticket allocation and sat on the bench with Harry Medhurst. I said I was one hundred per cent behind the players. And I went on television and had a go there as well. If Joe Mears had been chairman, I suspected it would never have happened. I think he would have sorted it all out in no time.

I couldn't understand why Mr Pratt had dug his heels in about it. Early on, we had seemed to be working together all right, in fact I had negotiated a new five-year contract with him and the board. But now the directors were naturally stung by my public state-ments.

We drew the tie at Brighton but before the midweek replay at our ground, I was summoned to a board meeting and asked to explain myself. The board said they took a serious view of my newspaper and television views. I could understand that, but I felt there were faults on both sides. I was given what I regarded as a fair hearing though, but I was officially given the slap-down.

We won the replay 4-0 but I wasn't in a mood for celebration. For the next day in the papers was splashed the revelation that I had been given a severe reprimand and warned about my future conduct.

The timing was incredible—the previous evening after the board meeting, I had walked past a group of newsmen, many of them friends of mine, as they were being given the official club statement by Mr Battersby. A few wry smiles came my way. I just felt low and humiliated.

You can imagine how I felt. When, if ever, had a manager received a public condemnation of his actions barely an hour before an important FA Cup replay? It may have been unique.

I thought it was ironic, too, at the time. The board, in issuing a statement to the Press, seemed to me to be doing precisely what they had accused me of doing—having a go in the columns of the media!

All sorts of wild things ran through my mind that evening. Even though we had won a place in the fifth round, I felt like getting in my car and driving away from Stamford Bridge for ever and leaving them to it. Then I thought: 'Why the hell should I? I've spent five years building a team—why chuck it all away now because of a few damned tickets?'

So I decided to soldier on. Row No. 1 had passed over. I little knew rows No. 2 and 3 were looming up! Normally, a run to Wembley is one of mounting excitement and joy. But underlying our progress to the great stadium in 1967 was the discontent over the board's attitude, and the entrenched position of the directors.

It was almost a stand-off and it flared up again when we beat Leeds 1-0 in the semi-final and it sank home that we were in the Cup Final for a confrontation with Spurs. Chelsea had never won the Cup, and had been involved only once before—way back in 1914-15 in a wartime atmosphere, when they lost to Sheffield United.

I wondered whether the board were as overjoyed as other groups of directors might have been in similar circumstances. For just over a week before Wembley, the players came to me with more grumbles. Yes, tickets had reared their ugly heads again, but on top of that, there were complaints about the bonus.

They had been told they could have 12 extra tickets each—two complimentary and a dozen to buy—for the greatest day in their lives. What was worse, they would get £50 appearance money, and only if they won would they receive a bonus.

If they were the victors, 19 players would share £12,000 between them. This incensed the players, because they felt they had been put in a position whereby they had to win to earn some reward for getting the club to Wembley.

They also knew that, in contrast, the Spurs men had been promised an impressive cash bonus whatever the outcome.

A Sunday newspaper somehow got hold of the story and on the afternoon before the Final, Mr Pratt told me he had denied it. To add fuel to the fire, the Chelsea players weren't informed of the precise details of the bonus until the eve of the game – hardly good mental preparation for such a great occasion!

I was as upset as the players. Once again, I had thoughts of packing it in. The players talked about a mass transfer request involving about 18 of them immediately after the Final, and also boycotting the official banquet. The air was fraught. Little wonder we lost the Final.

It was such a shame. We had won our way through to the semi-finals three years in succession, and – third time lucky – got to Wembley. That was quite an achievement.

And considering all the bickering in the background, once we got out there, our lads fought bravely before going under 2-1. Eddie McCreadie damaged his shoulder in the opening minutes and played under this handicap for much of the match, so we didn't have much luck.

All three goals bore a touch of good fortune about them and altogether it was a quiet final. Tottenham took a two-goal lead and got their 'killer' almost on half-time, always a bad time to concede a goal. Bobby Tambling got ours four minutes from the end but we had left it too late. Chelsea had to wait another three years – and next time they triumphed.

Despite all the discussed threats, we all duly turned up at the banquet. But the newsmen had sniffed it out and got their stories from various players, who were still smarting at what they regarded was a stingy attitude from the board.

The speeches droned on. When my turn came – and I was not on the official list of speakers – I let rip in a controlled sort of way, because I felt hardly any reference had been made to what the occasion was all about, an FA Cup Final.

We had played courageously and lost and I observed rather

sourly 'I was beginning to think that the people responsible for this club getting to Wembley—the players—were not going to get a mention.'

On the Monday after the final we flew off for the tour to the United States and Bermuda. The players were still seething with anger, and the newspaper stories let the country know it.

You'd think an end-of-season tour would be a nice way of winding down, but I was to fly straight into yet another rumpus, one which this time culminated in my saying goodbye to the club where I had worked in such happy circumstances for six years.

It all flared up in Bermuda and occurred through one of those incidents which seem trivial at the time, but which quickly develop into something far more serious.

We were playing a Bermudan side and winning 7-0 with about three minutes to go. Three minutes—that's all it took to force the parting of the ways with Chelsea.

A little coloured referee was in charge of the match. Suddenly, he ordered off Tony Hateley and Barry Lloyd. Now neither was hot-headed, and not surprisingly, they were reluctant to come off. I thought I had better get out there and try to sort it out. I would probably have persuaded them to come off as there was such little time left, and it seemed a minor matter.

The ref rounded on me and said tersely: 'Get off the pitch, white man.' I said 'What's that?' He repeated the phrase which I felt was a bit provocative to say the least. In fact, I saw red.

I had been called a few things in my time, but never 'white man' in that tone. I said the first derogatory thing that came into my head: 'You shouldn't be refereeing, you should be swinging from a tree.' That did it.

The summer weeks went by, the referee's report to the authorities back home came through, and the FA considered.

The 'beaks' didn't call me for my side of things. I felt I was tried and sentenced without a chance of explaining my version of the incident.

It was early in October, 1967 and the announcement came like a bombshell to me and Chelsea. I was suspended for a month. Apparently the FA had considered other remarks I had made while out there about refereeing standards and about the tour organisation which had called upon us to undertake three matches in three days—utterly ridiculous for an overseas tour at the end of a strenuous season.

Anyway, the implications were clear enough. I was not only barred from doing my job as manager, I was not allowed in the ground, not permitted to visit other grounds, and it was going to cost me £400 in wages—a lot of money in those days.

The FA probably also took into consideration my £100 fine for making ungentlemanly remarks to the referee after a youth game at QPR nine months previously.

This, of course, placed Chelsea in a real predicament. They could perhaps have done without me for a month, particularly as Ron Suart was then my No. 2. However, I talked it over with Mr Pratt and told him that in all the circumstances, and bearing in mind that things had deteriorated between us in the previous months, it might be best for all concerned if we parted company.

I had thought long and seriously about it. Things just weren't the same for me with Joe Mears no longer there with his rock-like personality which made my job easy.

So only a few hours after the news of the FA suspension broke, the papers had another sensation to get their teeth into—my resignation.

Mr Pratt told the Press: 'There was no pressure brought to bear on Mr Docherty, but I cannot say we were very pleased at the FA suspension. It was derogatory to the club.'

Six years is a big chunk out of anyone's life and I didn't know really where the road would lead me now. As it happened, and as in nearly every situation in which I had left a club for one reason or another, there was no shortage of offers coming my way.

Almost immediately, I received one from the Greek club Panathinaikos, who a few years later reached the European Cup Final under Ferenc Puskas and played at Wembley against Ajax.

The offer was a handsome one from the chairman John Pateras. Panathinaikos would pay me £10,000 a year from the moment my suspension period was served. At the same time, the wire was buzzing from Australia, and Karl Rodyn, the president of the

Hakoah club in Sydney, said they would be bidding for my services.

But though it was nice to contemplate a spell in Greece, I decided it wasn't for me and within a few days, I got a call from Jimmy Hill which I thought might well lead to me taking over at Coventry.

Jimmy had got Coventry to the First Division but was going into television. He phoned on the Monday to arrange an interview for me over lunch with Coventry's wealthy chairman Derrick Robins at Leamington Spa on the Thursday. But on the Tuesday night television news bulletin there came an announcement that Noel Cantwell was joining Coventry from Manchester United as manager.

Now Derrick Robins has been living in South Africa for a few years now—but I'm still waiting to hear from him! There wasn't a call, or any message of apology—nothing. Such is the way football clubs sometimes run their businesses.

Anyway, Jimmy was on the phone to me again only a few days later—obviously trying to be helpful in my hunt for a new job—and this time mentioned that Rotherham United were interested. The chairman, Eric Purshouse, he explained, was a little shy in making the initial approach, and he was doing it for him.

I said I would be interested. The next day I motored up to Yorkshire and had a chat with Mr Purshouse and his son Lewis. I found them nice people and we're still friends to this day.

I looked over the Millmoor ground and discovered that the facilities were good. It was November and the team were already struggling in the Second Division race, but I felt the potential was good. There was a keen set of players, who weren't greedy, money-wise.

One of my first signings was Dave Watson for £6,000 out of Notts County's reserve side. We had a useful run in the FA Cup, only losing out in the fifth round after two games with Leicester.

It was really refreshing to work with such a great set of lads like the goalkeeper Alan Hill, Neil Hague, Jim Storrie and David Bentley. There was a great family atmosphere and I immediately hit it off with the chairman, although the League results went against us.

It has been said that I spent a lot of money at Rotherham but that isn't true. I laid out a total of £43,000, including £25,000 for Quinn from Sheffield Wednesday and Storrie from Aberdeen for £7,000. But with sales I picked up £54,000, including £25,000 from Bristol City for centre-forward John Galley. And we made £29,000 profit from the Cup run.

It was also hinted that Rotherham players were paid too much money. I fixed a system of £25 per point, which I thought was good money at the time without being outrageous. The board was a small one, and one of the older members, Mr Ferguson, was a lovely old man who would go to the ends of the earth for Rotherham United.

Sadly, I couldn't stave off relegation, but there were no acrimony or recriminations. In fact, the directors insisted we all have a two-week holiday in Majorca – which at the time I thought was a magnificent gesture in the circumstances.

We had one or two little arguments, the chairman and I, but they were my fault. He was really as good as gold. He had a hard time understanding football people and what made them tick. He would say to me about referees 'How can men go out on the field on a Saturday afternoon and humiliate themselves for seven or eight quid a week?'

There was a lovely story attached to Eric Purshouse which I always think is worth relating. One day at Millmoor, Rotherham were murdering the opposition but were only level. Suddenly Jim Storrie broke through and there was the amazing spectacle of the home chairman shouting at the ref 'Offside – he's offside' about his own centre-forward. I think Mr Purshouse could see £25 bonus money going down the drain if Storrie scored!

Then after I had been at Rotherham only a year, the ill-fated offer from Jim Gregory at QPR came along and it seemed too good an opportunity to miss.

So I went to London, but in retrospect I often wish I'd stayed longer with those marvellous, friendly people in Yorkshire.

It was cruelly said that I left Rotherham in debt. That wasn't true. In fact, I left them some handsome legacies. I left behind me

Brian Tiler, a player who commanded a fee of £50,000 later, and Dave Watson, who went on to become the England centre-half and was sold for £100,000.

Watson always looked to me to have England potential. Indeed, I thought he was a better player at that time even than in his later days for England.

It wasn't the lure of London or the little extra money involved that induced me to return to the capital after only 13 months' absence. It was purely and simply that I found I couldn't resist the challenge of a move back to a First Division club to try to lift a struggling team—something I seemed to have been doing most of my life.

You could call me one of soccer's trouble-shooters, though I've no doubt my critics would say 'Don't you mean trouble-makers?'

The geography of the move didn't worry me, though I must admit that if you really asked me to choose to live in the north or in the south, I'd plump for the north.

I've never really had what I would call a home base, but in fact I loved living in London. Why? Because people were nice to me. One of the most often-repeated sayings about southern folk in England is that they are cold and distant. But I didn't find that.

I love going back to London, especially to rub shoulders with the taxi-drivers. They are great wits and I suppose the fact that I am easily recognised (because my old face has appeared from time to time in the papers!) made me something of a target. 'Oi, want a taxi, Tom?' is a cry I'm always hearing in the London streets.

I knew I'd made a ghastly mistake in leaving Rotherham as soon as I had been at QPR for a few days and, of course, as you know, I only lasted 28 days there. But there are times in life when you take a wrong turning. What really matters is that having done so, you get back on the right road as soon as possible and put that wrong turning behind you.

That right road led me to Aston Villa and another experience. But I shall never forget the warmth and outgoing nature of the folk in and around Rotherham. They say where there's muck, there's brass—but there's an outstanding kindliness among the people that's worth more than all the brass put together.

# 17
# Trauma With Aston Villa

THE OFT-USED description of me as one of soccer's trouble-shooters is apt. 'Whenever there's a mess to clear up, Call the Doc' seems to have been the watchword.

Nearly every time I have taken on a new managerial job, I have had to tackle problems such as re-organising staff, lifting the remaining players out of the doldrums and building them up to face new challenges, as well as trying to revive the club's flagging fortunes.

I like to think that in terms of Chelsea, Scotland, Manchester United and QPR I managed to achieve that in varying degrees.

One club, however, where I couldn't work the oracle, was Aston Villa. But to this day I firmly maintain that the reason was that I just didn't get enough time. Thirteen months is a ridiculously short space of time in which to put an ailing club in order, I think you'll agree.

Villa are not the only truly big club to pass through lean days after sampling the glory years. Tottenham, Sunderland, Newcastle, Chelsea, Sheffield Wednesday ... they've all tasted hard times when success seemed a very long way away.

Yet Villa are perhaps one of the very few who can compete, support-wise, with Manchester United and Liverpool.

It was a matter of great personal regret to me that in the short time I had in Birmingham, all I seemed to experience as a background to the playing, was boardroom wrangling, disillusioned crowds, and people who seemed hell bent on trying to run the club from the outside by pressurising the directors—not unlike the so-called 'junior board' at Old Trafford who never did anybody any good.

It's strange how fate can dictate sometimes how your path goes in a certain direction, and my association with Aston Villa is a clear illustration of this.

But for an accident, I probably would never have gone to Villa Park.

After my whirlwind 28-day experience at QPR, I was wondering what was next on my horizon when I got a call from an old friend of mine, George Sturrock. He and his son Richard had contacts in Spain, and were very friendly with, among others, Real Madrid. George told me Atletico Bilbao were looking for a coach and asked if I was interested.

I went out there and within a few hours, everything was more or less agreed, though nothing was actually signed. But while I was on my way home, the Bilbao president was killed in a crash.

While I was debating my next move, there came another call from another friend, Charles Tagwright, who was a great Chelsea supporter.

He knew Pat Matthews, who at that time was taking a very great interest in the shares at Aston Villa. Matthews was top man in the First National Bank, and wanted to see me about the possibility of me moving in at Villa Park.

This appealed to me so I saw Matthews and listened. It appeared that there was a strong chance that Doug Ellis, whom I knew as a Birmingham City director, might be the next Villa chairman. Matthews asked me if I knew anything about Villa's playing staff.

I rattled off a few names, some details about them, what they cost and so on. Matthews was impressed: 'For a chap who's not even been there, you seem to know a hell of a lot about them,' he said. 'It's our business,' I replied.

After establishing that I knew Ellis, he told me he might be the new chairman. That didn't bother me. He asked me what I would want to manage Villa. I told him a three-year contract, and specified salary and suchlike. 'Done,' said Matthews—just like that.

There was obviously a tie-up between Matthews and Ellis and within a few hours, Ellis and I were talking turkey.

Even at this early stage, there was a wee bit of friction in the conversation. 'Pat has told me what you want to manage Villa,' said Ellis, 'but I don't think we can afford that.' I was quick to the point. 'How do you know—you're not even chairman yet,' I told him.

'I was even asked what I thought of you as a possible chairman,' I added, 'but it was none of my business. I could have turned round and said I don't fancy you much as a chairman—you might not even get the job.'

That initial salvo over, everything was agreed. Ellis became chairman, a new board was formed. Harry Parkes, a former Villa full-back, joined and Harry Kartz was brought in. Harry Kartz is a super little director, and always one who could see the immense importance of developing a youth policy.

He's still on the board, and I was delighted for him as much as for anybody when Villa won the League championship.

But all the time I was there, turmoil seemed to exist at board level. They were always scuffling and diving about.

Doug was a good lad, but he was the big image man. And he was such a contrary fellow. He'd always feel he must disrupt the status quo.

He's the sort of chap who, if he'd been shipwrecked on an island, the first question he'd ask would be: 'Is there a government on this island?' If the reply was yes, he'd say: 'Then I'm against it.' That's his nature.

I remember a conversation when the team was having a sticky time. 'Don't worry, Tom, I'm behind you,' he told me. 'I don't want you behind me—I want you in front of me where I can see you,' I rasped back. 'That's the best place for directors.'

When I got down to the task, there was no real attention to youth at Villa Park. They'd actually sold their training ground.

So with the assistance of Peter Doherty, the old Irish international, and Arthur Cox, who helped me a lot, we got a youth policy going.

Doherty was not only a brilliant player in his day, but knew how to spot the right sort of youngster. He was also a great character. One of the first youngsters to join was Brian Little, who has since proved his worth for the club.

Another of the early decisions was to bring in Alan Bennett, who had been assistant secretary at Chelsea, as the club secretary. This was done on my recommendation because Alan had had experience of the big games and hectic ticket situations. In retrospect, I ought perhaps to have nominated Len Holmes, who was the secretary at Rotherham and who in my view was highly efficient at his job, better than Alan, who however, brought his experience to bear for a number of years afterwards.

The team was in a mess when I arrived in December 1968, but we managed to avoid relegation to the Third Division which at that time was a horrible spectre for the Villa fans who couldn't even stomach the prospect of staying long in the Second, let alone contemplating the disaster of falling into the Third.

Of course, it is history now that the drop to the Third did happen a few months after I was sacked.

We had to work hard to stay up in the remaining four months of that season and that meant players battling. This brought accusations from some quarters that we were using strong-arm tactics.

Bob Stokoe, the Carlisle manager, complained that we used 'diabolical tactics' at Brunton Park, and I had to warn him that he might get his fingers burned if he made any more public comments about Villa that could bring the club into disrepute. Anyway, we stayed up, and the *Birmingham Mail* used such phrases as 'Tommy Docherty has revitalised Aston Villa'.

So we started the 1969-70 season full of optimism, little knowing that things would get very shaky and that within a few months I would be looking for another job again.

Some even talked about us going back up that season, but instead we got off to a bad start. We lost an early home game to Leicester purely because Peter Shilton stopped everything we threw at him, and that was typical. We picked up only one point out of the first 10 and scored only one goal, and already the hounds were baying for my head.

One writer, Alan Hubbard, said that Villa were like a resprayed and renovated Rolls-Royce, standing at the kerbside and waiting to go places, but with the starting motor jammed.

Everyone was looking to us to do something, but things didn't improve.

As the season dragged on towards Christmas, the stories in the local papers increased in intensity, and around Villa Park the off-the-field critics were having a field day.

I brought in Vic Crowe to help me, but that was a mistake. Ironically, he got the job after I left.

With about 18 games to go, we were in the relegation zone. There was still ample time to get ourselves out of trouble, but the board panicked.

Doug Ellis told me 'We've given you a vote of confidence'. The dreaded words, I thought. I said: 'In that case, I'll go home and pack my bags, because that's the only thing you can do when directors give you a vote of confidence.' A week later, they sacked me.

This so-called confidence vote followed a long crisis meeting of the board which got blanket coverage on TV, radio and in the papers.

I had done everything I could to improve the results. I bought George Curtis, the Coventry centre-half who was a rugged and experienced defender, but everything that was done was against the background of this off-field ferment, which was bad for the team.

I'd been in other similar spots with other clubs, but never with quite the same sort of almost violent reaction from outside as there was round about this time at Villa.

When the big crisis meeting took place, I was kept waiting seven hours outside before I was called in.

The *Birmingham Post* commented that 'Since the great thing at issue was the club's play, for which the manager is primarily responsible, it is difficult to see how searching the meeting could be with Mr Docherty outside.' And they went on:

'Worse, of course, treatment of this kind diminishes his authority. If the manager is to be the man so completely responsible that it is his head that goes on the block when there is trouble, then the manager ought to be fully and obviously in the confidence of the board.'

I was in their confidence all right—for seven days. I told everyone I wouldn't resign because I was a fighter and always would be.

Curiously enough, at that precise time across the city, Birmingham City were having just as bad a time as Villa were and demonstrators were calling for the head of their manager, Stan Cullis. Stan and I had something in common over that period—but he, like me, had gone through it before.

I told the chairman I hadn't been given long enough to steer Villa in the right direction. And I actually offered to work for nothing for two years to enable me to prove I could do the job they took me on for. But that didn't cut any ice.

I could afford it at the time, but they'd obviously made up their minds, egged on by some people who had been putting the knife in.

Above it all, I felt Doug was a Birmingham City man and I think others around him on the board didn't really fancy a Birmingham man coming in and taking over the chairmanship.

But despite all the trauma and the in-fighting, I enjoyed my time with Villa.

I liked living in the Midlands. Villa had the aura of the big club about them. In my one and only summer there I made a forecast: 'Aston Villa will play in the European Cup one day.'

You had to be around at the time to understand how far-reaching a statement like that sounded, but though it took 10 years to come true, it has happened. And I'm very pleased.

For I've no hard feelings attached to Villa. Under happier circumstances, things would have been different. I was very sad when they went down into the Third at the end of that season. If only I'd been given more time...

But my New Year's present was dismissal. And I couldn't help reflecting back just over a year about how I might easily have gone to Bilbao instead.

Ronnie Allen took the job, and did a fine job. They won the Spanish Cup under him and he was a popular success.

Now it was my turn to go abroad and work—and no hitches this time.

# 18
# Lessons Abroad–then Home and Scotland

I SUPPOSE if you asked any footballer what was the highest honour he could attain, the reply you would get nine times out of 10 would be 'To play for my country'.

That was certainly true for me. And it was a wonderful bonus for me to be able to go on and captain Scotland after the thrill of my first cap in 1951.

But not in my wildest dreams did I ever envisage the time when I would become one of those very, very few people who have not only played for and captained their country, but managed the national team as well.

When I left Villa Park in January 1970 I was a bit down, naturally. But it's amazing how in life when one door closes, another opens. Even so, I would probably have laughed if you'd told me then that in just over 18 months' time, Scotland would say to me 'Would you like to be manager?'

In the meantime there were two other new experiences for me to undergo while I was in the domestic soccer wilderness, so to speak.

First, I tried my hand at football reporting. Through Bob Findlay, an old Fleet Street friend, I was engaged by the *Daily Mail* and for a while I went to matches and joined the writers on the other side of the fence.

Then I got an offer to coach the Portuguese club Oporto and away I went to the Continent–the first time I had taken a foreign appointment as a coach.

It was a very enjoyable experience and what was especially

gratifying for me, having 'run the gauntlet' between the board and the fans at Villa Park, was to see how the Portuguese supporters warmed to me.

It wasn't long before I realised there was one fundamental difference between the way they operate with players and conduct their financial matters, and the way we do it in Britain. I think we should give serious thought to using their system.

In Britain, it falls to the managers to involve themselves in the financial transactions between clubs, and to sort out players' salaries and so on.

Of course, managers can easily fall out with a player over his terms, especially if trying to keep within the club's budget. The player naturally thinks the manager is trying to deprive him, and a situation builds up between them.

But in Portugal, as soon as I'd arrived, they said: 'There are your players. You train them, coach them, and pick them. That's it. Any financial problems, we handle them.'

After seeing a few matches, I wanted one or two players, and pointed them out. 'We'll get them for you, Mr Docherty,' they said—and they did. I had absolutely no money dealings with those players. Whatever differences they had over cash, they had them with Oporto's financial director.

He knew exactly to what extent he could go, and the system left the manager to get on with his job without the added pressures of worrying about money matters. Terrific.

Isn't that something we should adopt in Britain, and wouldn't the managers be happy to have that awful worry off their backs? Of course. The pressures are heavy enough without the need to be wizard accountants as well.

There is one club where this is virtually done now—Queen's Park Rangers. There the chairman Jim Gregory does what the financial director does at Oporto—all the negotiating and fixing. And he does it well.

While I worked with him, if I wanted a player, he'd do all the bargaining. He'd agree the fee with the club, and agree the salary with the player. That for me was marvellous because if there was any falling out going on, it would be between the player and

Jim – and I would be outside it all.

If more clubs did it that way, we'd all be better off. Of course, the only problem is that it wouldn't be easy to find a director willing to take on all that responsibility.

The other main problem working abroad, of course, is the language barrier. The Oporto players understandably spoke little English so there was no alternative but for me to learn Portuguese. I had an interpreter friend operating with me for the first two or three months, while I went to night school and studied the language.

It was a different experience for me, but an easier one alongside the demands of the British game.

The players treated me with great respect. They always called me 'Mr Docherty'. They trained in the morning, occasionally in the afternoon, the climate was fantastic, and they played an average of about 30 games a season.

In fact, I trained them too hard to begin with and had to adjust my schedules, because I found their attitudes towards training were different to those found in Britain. You get the best out of them in other ways.

When they had their close-season, I took myself off to watch the World Cup games in Mexico in 1970, kept in touch with all the people in the game back home, and had some enjoyable days with the writers out there covering the finals.

Then it was back to Portugal, and I must say I thoroughly enjoyed every moment of my time there. But maybe back in England they were thinking about me and why I wasn't around any more.

For one day I got a phone call from the late Vic Railton, whom I always regarded as a fine journalist, and he told me they'd taken a poll in Manchester over who the fans would like to see as the next manager of Manchester United to follow Wilf McGuinness and I'd won it.

It was nice to hear this. But I reminded Vic that at this time, Harold Wilson had won a similar sort of poll over the Prime Minister's role, 'but he still isn't the Prime Minister' – and Vic laughed. Soon afterwards Frank O'Farrell got the job at Old

Trafford and my time was getting nearer—though of course, I didn't know it then.

But I wanted to come home at the end of my contract with Oporto, and even this is a smooth-running business out there.

When they know a coach is leaving, they bring in the new coach to work alongside him for the last six weeks or so, so that when the time comes for the take-over, he's well versed in what faces him. A good idea.

I wasn't back long before Terry Neill, who was boss at Hull City, asked me if I'd like to help him. It was nice to be wanted so I went there as his No. 2 and met up with the Hull chairman Harold Needler, who is one of the finest chairmen I have ever encountered.

Hull are now in the Fourth Division which is a crying shame, for they are a First Division club in terms of awareness and organisation. The city ought to have top-class football—it's a great pity.

Then came the approach from the Scottish FA to handle the national side on a trial basis, really to see whether they liked me, and whether it suited me. And over this period, Mr Needler continued to pay my wages at Hull, even though I was away on Scotland business for part of the time. That illustrated what sort of a man he was.

I knew Scotland had called me in to ginger the team up. They'd been having a lean time, and they'd little or no hope of qualifying for the later stages of the European championship.

You can imagine my feelings, even before the caretaker job turned into the permanent appointment—what an honour, what a thrill, to manage one's own country.

During the three matches of the trial period, I managed to pick the side up and the results began to improve. Ironically, we played Portugal at Hampden and beat them 2-1 with goals from John O'Hare and Archie Gemmill, and it was O'Hare who got the only goal when we also beat the Belgians at Pittodrie.

And we went to Amsterdam to take on Holland, who were a crack team at that time, and only lost in the last minute.

The Scottish FA gave me a free hand and the secretary Willie

143

Allen—a man who had taken a lot of stick in his time—offered me every assistance. There were no hard and fast rules laid down as to how I should tackle the job.

For instance, I don't think any manager of a national side can look upon his job as full-time. I think it's a case of putting in as much as you feel is necessary and it depends upon the individual.

I found the Scottish scene was dead and needed revitalising. The Scottish FA officials couldn't have been more obliging and I managed to get a cracking good squad together.

Altogether, we played 12 games during my time as manager, and lost only three. One of those was to Holland which I mentioned, and another was by the only goal against Brazil in Rio. In fact, on this tour of South America, we also drew with Yugoslavia and Czechoslovakia who were two of the best European sides.

I plumped for Billy Bremner as my captain straight away. I told him: 'Billy, you'll be skipper all the way to the World Cup.'

And as you know, Scotland went to Germany in 1974 and

---

### MY RECORD AS SCOTLAND'S TEAM MANAGER

| 13 Oct | 1971 v Portugal | Hampden Park | W | 2-1 (European championship) |
|---|---|---|---|---|
| 10 Nov | 1971 v Belgium | Aberdeen | W | 1-0 (European championship) |
| 1 Dec | 1971 v Holland | Amsterdam | L | 1-2 |
| 26 April | 1972 v Peru | Hampden Park | W | 2-0 |
| 20 May | 1972 v N. Ireland | Hampden Park | W | 2-0 |
| 24 May | 1972 v Wales | Hampden Park | W | 1-0 |
| 27 May | 1972 v England | Hampden Park | L | 0-1 |
| 29 June | 1972 v Yugoslavia | Belo Horizonte | D | 2-2 |
| 2 July | 1972 v Czechoslovakia | Porto Alegre | D | 0-0 |
| 5 July | 1972 v Brazil | Rio | L | 0-1 |
| 18 Oct | 1972 v Denmark | Copenhagen | W | 4-1 (World Cup) |
| 15 Nov | 1972 v Denmark | Hampden Park | W | 2-0 (World Cup) |

*Record:* Played 12, won 7, drawn 2, lost 3, 17 goals against 8

---

though they didn't get into the climax, they were the only side to emerge from the finals unbeaten. Even the winners West Germany lost one match.

I saw something of myself in Billy—a great little competitor and fighter. He had greater experience as a player than I had, and he'd played a lot more in Europe.

Having the pick of the players was like being a millionaire and being able to afford anything. I had Willie Morgan and Peter Lorimer on the wings, and both did a great job for me. If only I'd had Eddie Gray more often, for he was a wonderful professional with huge ability, but unfortunately he was dogged by injuries.

I was able to call upon players of the calibre of Asa Hartford, Archie Gemmill, John O'Hare, and that excellent centre-half Eddie Colquhoun.

George Graham, Martin Buchan, Sandy Jardine, Kenny Dalglish, Lou Macari—they all played well for me. I was spoiled for choice—there were others I could have called upon frequently like the Cropleys, David Harvey, Joe Harper, Pat Stanton—plenty of talent. I brought in Joe Jordan who was really still a kid then, and Kenny Burns.

One of the tragedies was that Bob Wilson, the Arsenal 'keeper, damaged his knee and went out of the scene. If we could have had a fit Bob Wilson, and a choice of Eddie Gray, Willie Morgan and Peter Lorimer on the wings, our full side, we'd have set the world alight.

I was on a four-year contract and I'd served only just over a year of it when the plum job at United was dangled in front of me—something that's always possible, I suppose, if you're having success as a national manager.

So Scotland and I parted amicably so that I could fulfil my long-term ambition and manage the greatest club of them all. Willie Ormond took over from me, and I can't say I thought much about the way he operated.

As soon as I got the United job, I wrote offering him any assistance he needed. Soon afterwards, we had a game against Coventry at Highfield Road and he turned up to watch big Jim Holton, our centre-half, and also Colin Stein, the Coventry centre-forward. He reminded me of my offer of assistance.

I advised him not to change the team around too much too soon otherwise the players who had done well under me might feel aggrieved.

In his first international against England on a snow-covered pitch, Scotland lost heavily. After that, Willie made his own choice, which he had every right to do.

I felt he didn't give the sort of attention to the job which I felt was absolutely necessary. I always did a lot of travelling and watching matches, and I made sure I was there the night before if there was a long distance involved.

But I remember Willie coming to one of our matches. He arrived 20 minutes before the kick off and went half an hour before the end, obviously intent on getting back to Scotland.

Every man does the job differently, but I couldn't see how that sort of thing could have been of much benefit to him.

Perhaps having got the momentum going, if that United offer hadn't materialised, and I'd stayed on with Scotland, we might have climbed tall mountains together.

But that's one of football's many 'ifs'...

# 19
# Hooligans—and a Confrontation

HOOLIGANS ARE the blight of football in Britain. A manifestation of the violent times we live in, and a festering problem which heaps bad publicity on a wonderful game that brings pleasure to millions.

We've all seen them in action, either on television, or with our own eyes at long-range, or close at hand.

But I must be the only manager in the business who was on the receiving end of a brutal, face-to-face confrontation with a group of them and who finished up in hospital with, among other injuries, 28 stitches in a leg.

As you might have guessed, I hit the front pages after they hit me. But what the nation didn't read about, as they shook their heads over this newest piece of hooligan behaviour, was the fact that while I was being beaten and kicked all over Stockport railway station, a famous international footballer sat only a few yards away from it all.

The date was Saturday, 8 December 1979 and I was the Queen's Park Rangers manager. We had played Wrexham that afternoon in London and drawn 2-2, and I was returning home on the train that evening. I'd had a meal on the way and I soon became aware of a noisy bunch of Manchester City supporters.

They'd obviously been to see City, who had lost at Ipswich that day, and their language was disgusting. Their behaviour to members of the staff on the train, including women, was shocking.

Having noticed me, they began singing dirty songs about myself and Mary. I went up to them and told them to be quiet.

They replied that I 'ought to be used to that sort of thing by now', and my reaction to that was to say to them 'Would you like to hear anyone singing that sort of stuff about your mother, for example?' They went very quiet.

I went back to my seat, but a little later they were starting up again. However, soon I'd arrived at my destination, Stockport.

About a couple of hours earlier, Denis Law, who was also travelling north and sitting a short distance away from me, had come up to say hello and we had passed the time of day.

As the train came to a halt and I put down my suitcase and leaned out of the window to open the door, I received a violent blow on the back of the head. As I turned round I could see this same group of City supporters were right on top of me.

There were about four or five of them and before I knew it I was on the ground and they were kicking hell out of me.

But I was on my own as the boots came piling in. There was a devil of a schemozzle with people shouting and screaming.

Only when the hooligans had gone off, leaving me lying there on the platform, did some of the other passengers come up and give me a hand.

Someone called the ambulance, and the police and Mary soon arrived. I was taken to hospital after being given oxygen on the platform. I was in hospital a week, and because of ruptured tendons in my knee, my leg was in plaster six weeks.

I wondered afterwards why no-one had stepped in to help me. Perhaps they didn't want to get involved. But I know one thing–if the situations had been reversed, or it had been anyone else–even someone I didn't like–I'd have been in there without hesitation. For me it would have been the natural thing to do.

As for the hooligans, they must have been taking it out on me because of the long-standing rivalry in Manchester between City and United, and because of my former involvement with United. Rivalry breeds emotions which can go to unnatural lengths.

I didn't really want to give evidence. I told the police they were wasting their time looking for the yobs because even if they found them, they'd be let off relatively lightly by the courts–and so they were.

None of them went to prison. Two of them were fined, one £250 and the other £50. A cheap price to pay for all my injuries, but not untypical of British justice—and the publicity made them local heroes.

For me, it was yet another example—and a painful, personal one at that—of the lenient attitudes the courts all too often take against hooligans who use football as their battleground, and tarnish the name of the game.

I was the first manager to get a personal taste of it, and I sincerely hope I'm the last.

The problem of hooliganism was very much part of my every-day life during the early 1970s, for over that period how could anyone be manager of Manchester United, and not be acutely aware of the seriousness of it all?

Yet, though the club got a bad name through the actions of a minority, it always seemed to be away from home that the trouble occurred.

We never seemed to have any bother at Old Trafford. Of course, one of the reasons was that where some of the other clubs had small numbers of hooligans following them, United, being a big, successful club with a world-wide name, could have had as many as a thousand.

And I'm sure that on occasions when we were travelling, fans at the other end put on red and white colours just to stir up trouble and this made things even worse.

Like the time we went to Norwich and fans wearing the red and white went on the rampage. It got blanket coverage on TV, and I was always suspicious of a set-up on this day. It smelled of being staged for the benefit of the cameras.

Why were they all there ready and waiting on that particular day, at that particular spot?

Thousands of words have been written, and hours and hours have been spent talking about the hooligan problem and so far they haven't come up with a proper solution.

But I've a suggestion that I reckon would bring it to a halt within 48 hours—bring back National Service and the birch.

I'm a believer in corporal punishment, and also the idea that prevention is better than cure. If the Government re-introduced National Service for everyone reaching the age of 18, and instilled discipline into young people's lives for a couple of years, as they did with myself and others for the few years after the last war, you'd see a marked difference in civil disorder.

And you'd see a difference if every offender caught making trouble at football grounds—inside or out—were to be given 10 strokes of the birch.

The do-gooders will raise their hands and howl. But look what their softness has led to in this country today. The worst thing we ever did was to stop National Service.

I did my two years and it taught me a lot. In fact it was the making of me. As a kid, I had the birch. I didn't like it, and I never wanted it again. They still retain the birch in the Isle of Man and the recent case in which it was used to punish an offender was the first in years. It's worked there and no mistake. There must be something in it.

The riots in our big cities are merely extensions of the violence that has afflicted football for years, but whatever Government is in power, they don't appear to be able to do anything about it.

To digress from soccer for one moment, I read that William Whitelaw, the Home Secretary, said the police would be having new helmets to help them face riots. What are new helmets going to do to solve the problem? Or hoses? But National Service would solve it.

At the moment, football hooliganism is just something we have to live with.

# 20
# The England Set-up

THEY SAY money is the root of all evil. And in my view it has certainly been responsible for some of the ills at top level in our national game.

It has certainly tarnished something which in my day as a player was beyond its dirty effect – being chosen for one's country.

I played 25 times for Scotland between 1951 and 1959 – and I wish it had been 50. For me, there was no greater thrill. And so it was for all of us in those days.

Nowadays – and I am speaking purely as far as England are concerned – for many players it doesn't seem half as important. Some of them don't even seem to care whether they pull on the white shirt or not.

Why? Because they're getting far too much money from their clubs and money has become their god. The prestige, the honour, the feeling you get when you hear that you're in the national side, has, for many of our so-called stars, lost its glitter.

I read the other day of a quote from the England wicket-keeper Bob Taylor, who had surprisingly lost his place to Alan Knott. It seemed as though he had a real axe to grind at being dropped. But what did he say? That it was one of those things, and he hoped he would soon be recalled because 'playing for your country is still a great honour'.

What an example from a cricketer to some of our soccer men. Not all, I hasten to say. Because thankfully some of them still place high value on an England call-up.

But many of them couldn't care twopence. You see them crying off from internationals when there's nothing really wrong with them. It doesn't mean anything to them any more. Isn't that sad?

At one time the money you received for playing for England was very helpful—it wasn't a lot, but it all went to making life a little more comfortable. Now some of these players are commanding so much money, they don't need extras.

I think this mental attitude applies almost exclusively to England, because international caps still mean everything to the Scots, the Irish and the Welsh.

So when people ask me: what's wrong with the England set-up these days, I give this as one of the answers—money.

Another prime reason is to do with the season, and its demands. Alone among all the big footballing nations, the English tolerate a programme of matches which is suicidal. And of course, the more successful a side is, the harder the season gets. And when a club wins more matches, it has more players called up for international duty, thus making it even harder. It's Catch 22.

All too often when England go abroad to play internationals—and for the most part these days they're either World Cup or European championship games, which are vitally important—the players are fatigued after a sapping season. And they're up against opponents who have had nowhere near as tiring a season as themselves. No wonder they cannot give of their best.

So these two major factors weigh heavily against any national team manager, whether it is Alf Ramsey, Don Revie or Ron Greenwood. Rather than being the supremo as their counterparts are in Brazil, Italy, Czechoslovakia and so on, they are just taking part. And we all expect them to be winners. Some chance.

All right, they have the pick of the players, though this doesn't always work out because of the players' attitude I have just mentioned. But how often has the England manager been unable to call upon key players because they're involved in an important club match?

It doesn't happen in other countries—they make sure the national team's demands come first and foremost, and everything else is subservient.

Until we in Britain adopt that attitude, we shall never be able to compete on a level basis with the other crack footballing nations.

All of which brings me to the third reason why I think England have struggled to find success.

Ron Greenwood is a very nice man. He's been treated as a nice man, quite rightly so. He had a marvellous record as England manager to begin with, until things began to go a little wrong and the criticism began to build up.

While I was out in Australia, I was reading about the England problems and about how Ron fell out with the Press. Now that's pressure—something Ron has never had to live with before to such an extent.

Having been a national manager myself, and tasted the very different pressures being in charge of your country brings, I can visualise exactly how Ron and the writers fell out.

Seemingly, there were stories that the players had virtually picked one England team. But Ron might quite innocently have said to two or three of the players 'How do you feel about playing with two wingers?' That is something that could so easily be misconstrued.

That would come back to the Press, probably from one or two of the players in the squad who weren't in the team and who felt they ought to have been and who had therefore a rather sour attitude. I can picture them saying quietly, 'You'll never guess what the manager has done...'

The next day, headlines: 'Players pick the England team.' Wham—Ron's unhappy. Wouldn't you be?

Of course, it is the job of the Pressmen to analyse and criticise and you can't blame them for doing their job when England are losing to teams like Switzerland in the World Cup, even after a long, hard season. If England hadn't won in Hungary, goodness knows what would have happened to Ron.

If I have one criticism of Ron, it is that he surrounds himself with too many coaches. Sometimes it looks as though there are more coaches than players.

The England job is really a two-man job—the manager and his No. 2. They should be able to cope with the full side and the Under-21s between them.

But Ron has had Dave Sexton, Bobby Robson, Don Howe and

Terry Venables. Many hands make light work, but in this instance I believe too many cooks spoiled the England broth.

So what does it add up to? A feeling that if you played for Manchester United, Ipswich Town, Arsenal and Crystal Palace, your chances of playing for England were that much better, because you would be seen more often by those running the national sides?

There might be something in this, because it would be human nature for anyone to pick the players whose skills he knows best.

But are they necessarily the best players? There might be young players just as good at Cambridge or Carlisle, but they get overlooked. Five or six men helping to pick the England teams should be able to see everyone, and they should at least appear to be fair. But are they?

If you've got too many people around you like Ron has, it can cloud your opinion and your judgment. You've got the best players in the country at your disposal. But with the exception of Bobby Robson and Don Howe, those people around him haven't been too successful.

Not only that, but the style of football that Don Howe has been successful with, as far as results go, would drive you mad from an entertainment point of view. I wouldn't cross the road to watch it.

I know Don quite well. Nobody was more open, attacking and inventive as a player than Don – not very good defensively, but terrific going forward, bags of flair. Now as a coach, he's almost the most defensive in the Football League.

If you look at his results, they're super. On paper, his record is fantastic. But people don't remember *how* some of the results were achieved. And if you watch Arsenal week in, week out ...

It's strange, because he's got and has had players of great flair. Arsenal had Brady, before he went to Italy, Rix, Sunderland, Stapleton before his transfer to Manchester United. He's got David O'Leary, probably the best centre-half in the world today, and a man who likes to go forward.

But too many players all over Britain today are coached not to lose. Coaches tend to protect themselves and their jobs by making sure they get results – but not in the way the fans like to see them achieved.

Alf Ramsey was another man who was a great attacking player himself, but regimented his side to such an extent that he did without wingers. England won the World Cup, and at the end of the day one always associates Alf with that terrific achievement. But what did it do for football to discard wingers?

You *can* achieve success with open, attacking soccer. Look at West Ham. They're a joy to watch. I'd go and see them every week if I had the chance. And Luton Town, and Ipswich Town.

The secret of West Ham's success you can trace to the attitude at board level. When they are relegated, they turn round and give their manager a fresh contract. For John Lyall, that was keeping faith in his principles, and hasn't he rewarded them since?

Other clubs, please take note. Those who want success tonight instead of tomorrow morning are stretching for the impossible. Give your manager time.

The trouble for England is that there is plenty of time, but the system clogs up the works. Now there's a new FA chairman, Bert Millichip, and a new Football League chairman, Jack Dunnett, my hope is that they can work out a solution that gives people like Ron Greenwood more chance to do the job they're paid for. Maybe then they'll get the results we all want.

# 21
# Managers—and
# Man-management

BRIAN CLOUGH would have made a successful England manager. But the Football Association didn't plump for him because he's too good at his job. That may sound like a contradiction in terms, but not when you examine the facts.

They didn't pick him because he's not a yes-man. They didn't pick him because he doesn't suffer fools gladly. And above all, they didn't pick him because he would have disrupted a few old diehard traditions in the cobweb corridors of Lancaster Gate.

He would have upset a few people and trodden on a few toes. But he would have put England right. That's the FA's loss. But sadly also, it's England's.

I must confess I like the man. He's a straight talker. He tells you what he thinks, and if you don't like it, he couldn't care less. But at least you know where you stand with him.

He has a marvellous record as a manager. I never argue with people's records—you can't alter the facts. People who say he's not a great manager don't know what they're talking about.

All you've got to do is examine his record with a no-hope club like Hartlepool, with Derby County, and with Nottingham Forest. He didn't stay long enough with Brighton or Leeds to be judged, and his short spell with Leeds is something akin to my first experience with QPR where it was obvious very quickly that things weren't going to work out.

He's good for the game. And he's a very generous man—he does a lot for charity. In times of trouble, he'd be the first man to come and help you.

In any list I was asked to draw up of the best managers of all time, he'd rate in the top three. My other two would be Bob Paisley and Jock Stein.

It's a toss-up whether Bob or Cloughie would come first; probably I'd go for Bob because of his incredible record at Liverpool.

You'll notice that all of them are modern managers—contemporaries of mine. There's a simple reason why, and it is this: compared with today, the managers of 20, 30 or 50 years ago had an easy time of it.

Never in the history of our game has so much mental and physical pressure been brought to bear on our managers as today through a number of factors.

The demands are enormous, and I don't only mean the long hours they are expected to put in. The standards are high, particularly with the growth of the world game, the season is longer, and they have a tougher time dealing with the players.

In the old days, players could be frightened by managers. Today managers have to deal with the super-stars, some of whom act like spoiled kids, and this calls for extra qualities, such as diplomacy, patience, understanding and so on. Then there's the fierce demand of extra competition.

In the old days there was just the League and the FA Cup. Now, on top of that for the big clubs, there's the League Cup and Europe. Europe brings its own different pitfalls, with managers having to plan and prepare for clashes with teams playing in different environments, with different tactics.

You just can't compare the job today with years ago. For men like Clough and Paisley, operating in the 1950s would have been a dolly.

The two men get their results in different ways, but in the final reckoning, what does that matter?

In terms of pure results, when you're talking about the best manager in Britain (for none of us knows enough about the rest of the world to throw the spectrum wider) you're talking about Bob Paisley. Then Cloughie, then Stein.

Some say Paisley inherited a great team from Bill Shankly. But it was just as hard to keep the momentum going. Not only that, he won three European Cups—there's no arguing with that.

Now when someone takes over from Bob, he'll have an impossible task. Cloughie came through the grade with Hartlepool. He almost made a silk purse out of them. But Bob came through the ranks as well.

He was a player with Liverpool, then trainer and was in Shanks' shadow for years. He's steeped in the traditions of Anfield, whereas Cloughie has had a few clubs. But he too has been an outstanding success.

Also on my short-list of all-time greats would be Matt Busby, Shankly of course, and Joe Mercer.

Matt would be there for more reasons than one—for what he's been through after the Munich air crash, for rebuilding Manchester United completely with Jimmy Murphy's help, and for making them great again.

Shankly and Mercer have got to be considered because of the way they handled their players. It's called man-management, and it's the real word to use when you're talking about the effects of coaching, and motivation and suchlike.

Coaching is a much mis-used and misunderstood word. People talk about coaching when they really mean forming a pattern of play.

Shanks and Mercer produced good players, and bought good players. They both produced the pattern of play they believed in, and after that it was down to man-management—not coaching.

Coaching is teaching kids how to play the game and making them understand the finer arts and the skills.

They talk about motivation. But what about when the manager needs motivating? Perhaps this is when the No. 2 comes into his own, when his boss is a bit down in the dumps.

These days, clubs are best run by a manager and a No. 2. And if the club is big enough, and can afford it, by a No. 3 as well.

I had Frank Blunstone and Tommy Cavanagh with me at United, and that was a good team. Cloughie has Peter Taylor and Jimmy Gordon with him at Forest.

At Liverpool, Ronnie Moran and Joe Fagan give the backing to

Bob Paisley. And I think it has become essential, because the pressure on managers today has become intolerably hard.

Joe Mercer is a classic example of a manager who gets the best out of his players with his manner and with his example. Even when he was caretaker manager for England in between Don Revie and Ron Greenwood, the players reacted to him and some of them said it was the happiest England squad they had ever known.

You've got to have a special quality to be a manager. That's why when Malcolm Allison was Joe's No. 2 at Manchester City, things went well and they won everything. When Malcolm branched out on his own—no good.

I've never been under Malcolm so I can only relate what I hear about his coaching. I'm told he's very good at it. But as a manager—a disaster. I don't think Malcolm has ever realised what he's really good at. He would like to have been a good manager, but never made it.

I always think that good coaching can be summed up in this way: that if you're a player, and you like and enjoy the way you are handled, that's good coaching. Coaching isn't about running and arranging free-kicks—that's organisation.

Coaching is getting hold of young players and producing them up to a standard where you can go on and make them League players. Ability and hard work will do the rest. That's what Cloughie does so well.

Down the years, I have often been put in the same category as Malcolm and Cloughie: but that's because we are men who make decisions.

When you make decisions, sometimes you upset people. And when you upset people, you sometimes fall out with them, and that makes headlines. That's why we are cast in the same mould.

Also we are constantly in the news because we are said to be outspoken. That's because when we are asked our opinion, we express it.

If people don't like the opinion, it's usually because it's the one they didn't really want to hear. So right away, we're criticised for voicing that opinion.

So I guess you can say that the three of us are in the same bracket. I think I have had more car crashes than Malcolm, and certainly more than Cloughie because he is driven around by somebody else. I don't know, either, who drinks more champagne. Probably Cloughie because he's had more success than Malcolm or myself!

You may think me swollen-headed for saying it, but I think the game needs characters and personalities. We are in the entertainment business, after all, aren't we?

I think the game needs the quiet men like a hole in the head. The silent men do nothing for the game.

Maybe we talkative ones are a bit much sometimes, maybe not. Mind you, they say Bob Paisley's a quiet man – but he isn't really, you know.

When Bob has something to say, he says it – and it's usually straight to the point. So far as Bob's concerned, I've never known Liverpool to be well beaten yet. When they lose, Bob wants to hold a saliva test for his players.

Now there must come a time for any manager when you hold up your hands and admit: we were well beaten. Not so with Bob. I think a bit of this attitude rubbed off Bill Shankly on to Bob. So don't call him a quiet man – at least, only quiet in comparison with me, Cloughie and Malcolm.

In considering the great managers, you're also bound to think of Alf Ramsey. He won the League championship at Ipswich when they were a 'nothing' team by the yardstick of today's great Ipswich side, and they knighted him for leading England to victory in the 1966 World Cup.

The more I got to know Alf, the more I liked him. I had a few dealings with him when I was Scotland manager. He knew the game inside out, and he was great with his players. They'd walk to the ends of the earth for him.

He had a reserved attitude towards the media, though he got on well with some of them. Perhaps he didn't trust them – and he might have had good cause for that.

We are all made differently. While Alf was wary, I have always adopted the approach with the Press that if you are asked a sensible question, you provide a sensible answer. If the question is stupid, well, maybe that deserves a stupid answer. But you have always got to give an answer, even if it calls for you, on the odd occasion, to say 'Piss off.'

When you're discussing managers and management in today's hurly-burly, it should be said that the boss is often as strong as the men he's got alongside him. These blokes are the unsung heroes of football, the men who very rarely get even a mention, let alone any headlines to themselves. The Tommy Cavanaghs of this world. What would we do without them?

Tommy and I have been friends since 1949 when I met him in the railway station in Preston after I had come from Glasgow. We played in the reserves at North End together, but he was transferred to Stockport County after one or two games in Preston's first team.

Even when we haven't worked together, we've always kept in touch. One of the first phone calls I made when I began my job back at Preston this summer was to Newcastle to congratulate Tommy on joining another old colleague of mine, Arthur Cox, on Tyneside.

Tommy was out of football when I started helping Terry Neill at Hull, so we took him on as one of our coaches. And when I was in charge of Scotland, he even spent his holidays helping me out with the national squad, and eventually I took him from Hull when I was at Old Trafford.

He did a great job for me and stayed on when I left there in 1977, but even his head rolled when Dave Sexton was sacked this year. And that surprised me.

For Dave couldn't have been an easy man to work with. He and Tommy make a total contrast in personalities. Dave is a quiet type of fellow, but Tommy is hard, and drives people.

Tommy would become a little bit disliked for the simple reason that if the manager's not wielding the stick, he's got to wield it himself. So Tommy did, and in my view the club had much to thank him for.

He'd been at United over eight years and done a fine job. In the circumstances surrounding Dave's departure, with Ron

Atkinson only replacing him weeks later as far from first choice, I would have thought they would have kept someone like Tommy on in the meantime, to hold the fort, so to speak.

One of the hard facts about life in a big football club these days is the mass sacking of the back-room staff which often takes place when a new manager comes in. I know it appals people and what happened at United was a case in point.

In this instance, Tommy Cavanagh, Harry Gregg, Jack Crompton and Laurie Brown all got the push, largely because Ron wanted to bring his own staff in.

However, there are two sides to this business. I have always given the staff I have inherited a chance to prove themselves, with the exception of bringing in my own No. 2 immediately.

At United, I kept men like Laurie Brown because they had done a good job for the club, so why get rid of them?

But incoming managers invariably feel that by bringing men in whose capabilities they know inside out, there is more chance of harmony and success than in starting from scratch with existing staff to whom they are strange faces. And you can understand that point of view, harsh though it is on the men who are being kicked out.

On the other side of the coin is the feelings of those men who might have given years of devoted service, like Dave Ewing did at Manchester City only to find he was out of a job when John Bond arrived.

Take Laurie Brown, too. He can look back on the United ins and outs, and say in all honesty 'I can't be out because of my work, because the new man hasn't seen me working.'

This can also be said by Harry Gregg and Jack Crompton. But then United's back-room staff is big enough already without keeping the old faces on as well. So in a way, they would be surplus to requirements.

Football is a peculiar business, because in most other jobs, the sack is a stigma. But in soccer, you can often say: 'I've worked very hard, I've done nothing wrong, yet I've been pushed out.'

The new manager has brought in his own physio, but the

outgoing physio might be better at his job. You could argue a strong case for unfair dismissal in an instance like this.

Don't forget, managers too can be the victims of what might be termed unfair dismissal. But how many of them take it to an industrial tribunal?

This is where I think the Secretaries and Managers Association should get their priorities right, and get down to the nitty-gritty of protecting their members' rights and privileges instead of huffing and puffing about trivialities.

Suppose you are appointed to a manager's job and you sign a five-year contract worth £100,000 and after 12 months you get the sack, you don't necessarily get an £80,000 cheque. What the club might then say is 'See your solicitor,' so you've got to battle for what you can get. And at the end of the day, the club might ask you to sign a piece of paper promising not to speak to the Press or you won't get the money they've agreed with you. That's a form of blackmail.

If you take the fight into court, you might, if you're lucky, get the amount you're seeking, plus a bill for £10,000 legal fees.

I'm not saying this happens all the time. But it is an example of how difficult things can be for a sacked manager if the club wants to be awkward.

So in my book, the Secretaries and Managers Association should get down to it.

They should seek, and get, an agreement from the Football League clubs that if, for example, a man gets the sack and is owed £10,000 or £100,000 for the remainder of his contract, it should be fully paid up. That's what they do on the Continent, and that should be good enough for us over here.

Conversely, there should also be a clause in every contract whereby if a manager leaves a club through his own initiative, or through the overtures of another club, the club he is leaving must be fully compensated for the remainder of that contract. It should cut both ways. If this were done, there would be far more honour and trust in the game.

The situation that exists now is a joke. A contract isn't worth the paper it's written on. Both parties can point a finger at each other at present and find faults and flaws. Look at how angry West Bromwich Albion were at losing Ron Atkinson.

Both parties have got to be protected if there is to be any sanity. It's time something was done, and who better to get it done than the Secretaries and Managers Association. They carry the weight.

It might even be said that it's better to work without a contract. Jack Charlton has done it for years. But I would only take this on if I had a million pounds in the bank, or if I felt I was financially well enough off not to worry about getting the chop.

If you work without a contract, and you get the sack after a couple of months, you get nothing. If you are shoved out after 18 months, and you've got a contract, at least you get something to pay the bills with.

I don't think anyone really enjoys working without a contract, except those who are financially secure anyway, or who are backing their judgment until such time as they get a good offer from another club, when they can turn round and say 'There's no compensation to pay, so you can give me a bit more for myself.'

On the vexed subject of contracts, there's food for thought...

# 22
# Players and Attitudes

I HAVE HAD the privilege of being in charge of many great players in my time – some of whom I bought. But I make no apologies for kicking off this chapter on players by mentioning Philip Nutt.

Now outside a few Queen's Park Rangers supporters, I don't suppose anyone has ever heard of Philip.

Philip was a defender, a centre-half or a full back. His ability, his attitude, his make-up were all wonderful – the sort of combination a manager dreams about. But poor Philip was plagued by injury and had to quit the game at the tender age of 21.

That sort of thing hurts me more than anything else in the business, when I think of the players who have so much ability, but who have completely the wrong attitude towards the game.

You can talk to players like this until the cows come home, but it doesn't make any difference. But there comes a stage when you say to yourself: I've gone as far as I can go, I'm wasting my time.

The worst thing to deal with, I think, is the player who will not always give of his best. If he puts his mind to it, he can be the best player on the park, probably score a hat-trick. Other times he wouldn't bother all that much.

Another type to cause managers problems is the barrack-room lawyer – the player who kicks against the off-the-field discipline.

Two of these I had at Derby: Bruce Rioch and Don Masson. Both were excellent players – but they'll both agree with me that we had our off-the-field differences.

Bruce I bought twice – once for Villa, when I signed him and his brother from Luton, and once for Derby when I bought him from Everton.

I had a high regard for him as a player, for I'd picked him for

Scotland earlier, but that was at the time when he was making up his mind whether to play for Scotland or England. Eventually, of course, he plumped for Scotland.

But like Masson, he became a barrack-room lawyer. It's surprising in view of my experience with them both to see them now aspiring to management positions, Don with Notts County, and Bruce at Torquay.

I suspect now that they'll have to change their views, and they'll both probably realise that what I and other managers did, which they didn't agree with at the time, was right.

I like Bruce as a fellow, and I liked him as a player, but, at Derby especially, I was bitterly disappointed with him as a professional.

I found that another famous Derby player of that time, Roy McFarland, also disappointed me as a pro. Again, he was a great player.

At one time, Roy was probably one of the best centre-halves ever to play the game but I must say I had a few problems with him. Long before I went to the Baseball Ground, I fancied him as a player and would have liked to sign him for United, but as it turned out, I was lucky in that I think Martin Buchan turned out to be just as good a player.

Roy had a good testimonial with Derby and while I was there I had offers for him—one, I recall, from Wolves—which I turned down, simply because he was a magnificent centre-half.

We fell out over a free transfer which the board and I refused to give him.

He didn't like that decision, and he's said a few hard things about me since I left Derby.

Unfortunately for Roy, for a long spell he was never fit. He'd always be suffering from pulled muscles and consequently not be available. Fitness is essential for footballers, and I am always sorry for those who have fitness problems.

I don't want to give the wrong impression. The disappointments and disagreements I had with players were few compared to the large number of splendid pros who worked with me down the years.

I have been very fortunate with the players under me. Many of them were hand-picked of course, but all of them knew me and what was expected of them. They knew they could have a good time with me on occasions, but also knew how far they could go.

They were well aware that if they tried to con me, they'd be on their bikes double-quick. The Chelsea boys who stayed out at Blackpool overstepped the mark and I had to take action.

The player–manager relationship depends to a very large extent on the attitude of the player towards the club rules, and how the manager reacts when they are contravened.

I never hesitated to fine players when they broke the rules, in fact I did quite a bit of it through the years, and only occasionally did news of the fines leak out.

It cost Bruce Rioch £450 in 1978 when he took himself off during a game with Newcastle, and we subsequently had a row about it. I had occasion to suspend Don Masson for a fortnight without pay the same year. He'd already been fined £500 for missing a pre-match meal!

The manager has got to act sometimes when the rules are abused. Maybe he's the bad egg in the eyes of the players–but if they hadn't broken the rules in the first place, there would have been no problem.

Mentioning that, I recall Eddie McCreadie once saying to me some time after the Blackpool incident: 'I used to idolise you. It was an honour to walk down the street with you, until you sent us home from Blackpool.' My reply was: 'You were the one who went down the fire escape–not Tommy Docherty.'

Years afterwards, I met him at Chelsea when he was their manager just after they won their way back into the First Division. We had a drink together, and he looked a bit thoughtful.

'Do you know, boss' he said–and even after all those years he still addressed me as 'Boss'–'you were right to do what you did at Blackpool.'

'I know I was right, Eddie,' I told him. 'There was nothing clever about it. It's just experience.'

There are times when a manager has got to be unpopular. You've got to handle different players different ways. Some you give a rollicking to, in order to get the best out of them. Others you have to coax along.

Each club that you go to brings you a new set of problems. And the stimulating part of managing or coaching is that those problems are never really all solved. As soon as you are sorting one out, another unbeknown to you, is arising elsewhere, and you'll soon have to face it. It's a continual challenge.

You will always make enemies. You may think a man like Dave Sexton, who is a nice fellow, could never upset anyone. But maybe, somewhere along the line, he's upset players by ignoring them, by not talking to them just as I've upset them by talking to them a bit abrasively. Dave might upset them by not making a decision, while I do precisely the same by making a decision.

Handling players is very much a personal thing. The fans always seemed to have the impression that Peter Osgood was a prickly individual to handle. Not a bit of it – for me he was a piece of cake.

If ever Ossie got stroppy with me, I'd say to him 'Aw be quiet, shut your bloody face, come on, we'll have a bottle of wine.' He was a super lad – I knew what I had to do and he responded.

Other managers might have acted very differently – I may have done myself a long time ago, but that's where experience comes in.

Norman Hunter and I were never on the same side together, always adversaries. We used to swear at each other, he from the field, I from the bench. The only reason I didn't like him was that he was always a damned good player against me, nothing else. But we'd always smile and joke about it afterwards.

That's the spirit of the game which people outside don't see. All they maybe heard was the odd swearword and thought there was bad blood!

Some players would say silly things after our association had ended, but I rarely took them seriously. One such comment was from Gerry Daly who reckoned we couldn't stand the sight of each other.

Now Gerry can speak for himself. But for my part, I can stand the sight of Gerry because he was a good player – but unfortunately he talked to the wrong people and I thought he went downhill after he left Manchester United.

That was a sort of Irish quote from Gerry. He came to United from over the sea and was very promising. But he was always a 'Fancy Dan' type of player with not a lot of grey matter.

He asked for a transfer because he was left out of the United team, but at the time we were playing two in the middle of the park instead of three, and McIlroy and Macari were better players. I think he was pushed into it by his wife.

I fined him once or twice at Derby later because he was out until about two or three in the morning on the day of a match.

He was on a lot better money at United than he was in Ireland, and I also fixed him up with a great contract to go and play in America.

So for a fellow who can't stand the sight of me, I've put a hell of a lot of money his way. But as I say, you don't pay too much attention to what lads like Gerry say – you just do your job and get on with it.

On the good side, I can reel off many names of men I have been proud to work with, and who have been wonderful pros and a credit to the game.

It's astounding how so many of the players who have comparatively limited ability are the best professionals, because they have to work at it, whereas sometimes the men with the most natural ability, are the ones who run into trouble and disappointment, wasting and neglecting their talent because of a deficiency in their make-up.

What's between a man's ears has been put there by nature – you can't alter it.

Some of the men under me at Old Trafford were terrific pros – Brian Kidd, Buchan, the two Greenhoffs, Steve Coppell, David McCreary, and Arthur Albiston. Also Alex Stepney, Willie Morgan and Ian Storey-Moore whose career was cut short by injury.

At QPR, I found similar co-operation and team-spirit from such as Glenn Roeder, Clive Allen, Paul Goddard, Don Shanks and Stan Bowles.

Roeder was so intense that I once had to pull him off in a match at Sunderland because he had been booked, and he was getting too heated and too involved, and I brought him off to save him from possible further action from the referee – but he was a dedicated pro.

At Rotherham, I can safely say I didn't have a bad pro, and Dave Watson was always 100 per cent for me. At Villa, I always had great regard for goalkeeper Jake Findlay, who has since been with Luton. Going further back to my Chelsea days there were several – Peter Bonetti, little Tommy Harmer, Frank Blunstone, Bobby Tambling, Barry Bridges, John Mortimore, the Harris brothers Ron and Allan, and yes, Terry Venables who was a good pro even though he was 'King of the Kids.'

Jimmy Greaves had almost a child-like attitude to his work. To Jimmy, the whole thing was just a game – he never took things seriously. In training matches, he would always want to play in goal, even though he was the greatest goal scorer of the age. A genius at his trade.

Then there were the opponents. I had always wanted to buy Peter Shilton but never managed it. I would love to have Kenny Dalglish playing under me, and Eddie Gray who had a marvellous outlook towards the business.

Johnny Giles and Johnny Haynes – what passers of the ball. World-class. At Leeds I always had plenty of admiration for Bremner and Hunter. Without meaning anything nasty I couldn't help wondering if Norman had developed conning referees off to a fine art. Mind you, all the Leeds team looked good in this respect. They were so competitive.

Players are, after all, a reflection of life itself. You get all sorts, shapes and sizes and temperaments.

It wouldn't do for them all to be the same. If that were the case, life for us managers would either be deadly dull and bore us all into the grave, or be so harum-scarum that we'd all finish up in a sort of football asylum.

I'll settle for it the way it is. But I often wish I had started out with the experience I gained along the road. It would at least have saved me a lot of heartache!

# 23
# A Question of Leadership

FOR MANY years—even though the evolution of the game has taken its natural course and kept pace with the developing trends—the butchers, bakers and candlestick-makers who comprise the Football Association continue to trundle on their weary way. But their day is fast coming to an end.

It seems hardly conceivable to us today that only a matter of 30 years ago, the amateur businessmen who occupied the powerful seats at Lancaster Gate were still putting their heads together to pick the England team!

All that, thank goodness, has changed and now the professionals are doing that job. But the men with the power are still very much amateur enthusiasts. And however much you praise them for the time and interest they put into it, we are rapidly approaching the 21st century and it has all become somewhat outmoded.

The time for a professional—a man who has been through the mill either as a player or a manager or a full-time administrator—to take the top post at the FA is almost here.

And I have no hesitation in saying that one man who would be a fine chairman of the FA one day soon would be Jimmy Hill.

Jimmy has done it all. He's been a professional player, a union negotiator who spearheaded the fight to remove the shackles from the players' wages, a manager, a coach, a TV soccer personality, and more recently, the chairman of a First Division club. What person better suited to know what every major aspect of the game is all about than he?

I wasn't sorry to see Sir Harold Thompson stand down. I thought he was a bit of a joke as FA chairman. His successor, Bert

Millichip has at least shown he is a very able man in handling disciplinary matters and I wish him well.

But just as Matt Busby moved from the playing and managerial side of the game to the administrative side when he became a director at Manchester United, and exerted great influence on the club's destinies, so I believe Jimmy would be able to do the wider job as FA chairman.

I have had very few close dealings with him. I remember selling John Sillett to him when I was at Chelsea and he was building the Coventry City team up from nothing in the early 1960s.

But one has to admire what he has done, the fair way in which he approaches every topic, and the impression he never fails to give that he is trying to get the best deal for everyone – the players, the clubs and the spectators.

He's been good for the game. He instituted a lot of ideas while he was at Coventry that were laughed at during that period, but as soon as people elsewhere saw they not only worked, but earned money and pleased the fans, they copied them.

He may well not have figured the transfer market would go to such stupid lengths when he quite rightly fought on the players' behalf all those years ago. You could even say he has ironically brought it upon himself now that he is a club chairman and has to deal with players' wage demands from the other side of the fence, so to speak.

But he has been such an able negotiator, that he should be able to find a way around this sort of problem, just as he has overcome other hurdles in his extraordinarily varied career.

If Jim were in charge at Lancaster Gate, the one thing he wouldn't do would be to wait for an annual meeting each year to get things done.

He's not the sort of man to sit around and talk about things but do nothing about them. If there were something worthwhile to do, you could be sure he'd be all for putting it into practice, or at least trying it, at once.

At the present time, the corridors at FA headquarters are still festooned with cobwebs. The powers that be wouldn't be too happy about someone like Jimmy taking charge.

They don't want too many intelligent people, particularly from the professional side, horning in on their preserves. If that happened, the game would take off–they desperately want it to remain as it is, because if it changed, that would mean they would have to work harder and this would expose them. Bright ideas are the last things they look for.

But it will have to come. They're a dying breed. They have done their bit in the past, but times change. The game's become too big and too important for a bunch of well-meaning but archaic amateurs to go on holding the reins for ever.

So I look forward with relish to the day when Jimmy–or someone like him with the modern approach and the good of the game at heart–takes charge.

I'm sure he's a great chairman to work under, because he understands what it's all about, from top to bottom.

But, of course, he's a rarity. Other chairmen of Football League clubs are non-professionals. They are 'amateur' enthusiasts.

Like all directors, they put a tremendous amount into the game and often get unfairly abused.

I often relate an anecdote that every club should have three directors–two dead, and one dying. But, by and large, directors put a hell of a lot more into the game than they get out.

I am a fortunate man, for with few exceptions, I have been blessed, during my 20 years of being a manager, with good and understanding chairmen.

Let's just run down the list and put the Docherty microscope on them:

*JOE MEARS*–my chairman at Chelsea in the early 1960s. A magnificent club leader. Very difficult to find a better chairman. Very firm and very strict, and I knew exactly how far I could go with him. Always I would get a decision from him–yes or no, and not always the one I liked. I always said if he had continued as Chelsea chairman and not been forced to stand down because of ill-health, my time at Stamford Bridge would have been greatly extended.

*ERIC PURSHOUSE*–he was chairman during my time at Rotherham. A smashing man and easy to work with. Curiously enough, he wasn't what you would call an out-and-out football fan. In fact, he really wasn't deeply interested in the game—just in seeing Rotherham do well. A very funny man, and with a great sense of humour. Any time I spend in his company is happily spent. A nice guy.

*DOUG ELLIS*—I have touched on Mr Ellis in an earlier chapter. He was all right, a trifle egotistical, I thought. He wanted to be king, but he had a contrary nature.

*HAROLD NEEDLER*—a great family man and a wonderful chairman of Hull City for many years. He loved the game, and in the few months I was at Boothferry Park, he and I found we had one thing in common—we both hated referees (not really, Clive!).

*LOUIS EDWARDS*—a lovely big man whom I had tremendous respect for and to whom I devoted a whole chapter early in this book.

*GEORGE HARDY*—in the end he had a rough ride at Derby because others wanted him out of the chair, and succeeded in the end. I found him okay a lot of the time, but his trouble was that he tried to please everybody—an impossible task in a hurly-burly business like football. He should have been stronger and would have been chairman today if he had been.

*JIM GREGORY*—again, I have already mentioned my association with him at QPR. The relationship with him has got to be unique, for the money a manager is spending is actually Jim's, so you can't blame him for wanting a big say in how it is spent. While my other chairmen have all let me get on with the job, Jim did that only as long as we did it together!

Everything had to be done with his blessing—but that's not a criticism of him. I probably learned more from him than any other chairman in terms of wheeling and dealing. In the final reckoning, after having had three spells under Jim, I got a raw deal—that's my honest opinion. But I have no bitterness over it.

He's a smashing man and a character—and if I bumped into him tomorrow we'd shake hands, have a drink and a good old chinwag.

*JIMMY AITKEN*—this is a name that may not be well known in England. Jimmy is at Partick Thistle and while I was Scotland manager, he was president of the Scottish FA and I shall always be grateful to him for the help and co-operation he gave me. We got on well.

I learned enough in my association with all these men to know one thing for sure—the manager's ideal situation is to have a strong, powerful chairman with whom he has an understanding, and who has his directors in line with his thinking.

There are times when you would like to keep all the directors in touch with what is going on, but the trouble is that things happen so fast in soccer, especially in transfer deals, that there just isn't enough time to go through all this rigmarole. That's when you want the chairman's nod and away you go and do the business. The others can be told afterwards.

So generally speaking, I say: thank you gentlemen. We both did our best.

# 24
# Referees, TV and Other Facets

REFEREES and television are two totally different areas of our national game, yet because of the effect of the exposure of the former upon the latter, they have become intertwined. And for the most part, the poor old much-maligned referee has emerged with his image tarnished rather than enhanced.

Yet one of the oldest cliches in the business still stands good for me today—the British referee is the fairest, the straightest and most honest of any in the world. Never, I believe, would a British ref set out deliberately to cheat anyone, and that cannot be said for refereeing everywhere, because I have seen plenty of it straight out of a horror comic.

So every Saturday, as a manager, I expect—and I get—a standard of refereeing which is of the highest order. And despite our moans and groans about individual decisions, that remains true. But I must admit there is one ref who never ceases to puzzle me—and that's Clive Thomas.

Clive is a great referee, of that there is no doubt. He's one of the best in the business, and by that I mean world-wide. But why does he have this unfortunate knack of attracting controversy?

It's almost as if he's thinking 'If the game's going well, I've got to do something to stop that.' Despite all his experience, he has never managed to keep out of the news for long.

We all have our personal memories of a Clive decision that has gone against us. I particularly recall on important Cup game when I was at United and we lost 1-0 to Southampton to a goal that must have been offside in my view, five or six yards. Saints won deservedly but the fact was that Clive let the goal stand—so one remembers him for that.

Perhaps the most famous example of Clive attracting attention to himself was the 1981 League Cup final between Liverpool and West Ham. He allowed a Liverpool goal which afterwards, by general agreement, was proved to be offside.

Okay—that can happen. But when John Lyall protested afterwards, Clive tried and judged him before his own report even went to the Football Association.

I'll say this for Clive—he's consistently controversial. Yet he's a top-class ref. As I say, with all his experience, why he should continue to be always the ref in the limelight puzzles me.

I used to have a few problems with referees when I was younger, both as a player and a manager. But I have gradually learned what I should have learned at the outset—that refs are only human, doing a difficult job as best they can, and you just have to accept their decisions. There's nothing you can do to alter them.

I think it is true that over the course of a year decisions do level themselves out. But you always tend to remember the ones against you that rob you of something, rather than the ones for you which rob the other team. I guess that's human nature.

I don't line up with those who think that full-time professional referees would make any difference to the standard in Britain.

The first problem to overcome would be: is there enough work for them to turn full-time? I doubt it. They'd train every day, but would they be any fitter than they are now, or what's more to the point, would full-time training make them better referees? Again, doubtful.

Most of them already have jobs where their employers are very good to them and give them ample time off.

I think there are ways of making referees more efficient and more proficient, but they don't necessarily entail them becoming full-time professionals.

For example, I like the idea in West Germany where the referee and his two linesmen travel together regularly. Not surprisingly, in this they get to know each other very well and their teamwork becomes well nigh perfect. I think that could be attempted here.

There is one area of our game where I don't fancy you'd be able to get any improvement—or hardly any—and that is in the coverage by television. We are fortunate to be able to boast a standard of commentating and production which must be second to none anywhere in the world.

John Motson and Brian Moore—and possibly Barry Davies too—are unequalled anywhere. They're not only brilliant at their job, they're also very fair, and that is very hard to achieve when they must get caught up in the emotion of it all as we all do.

Both the BBC team under Jimmy Hill and ITV's squad under Brian Moore are absolutely first rate.

The Germans are good at it too, because like us they have the facilities. But in my view, our coverage is the tops, particularly the presentation, and we are lucky that the standard is so high. I have some experience of the coverage in Australia and of course what they lack in comparison with our game is the atmosphere surrounding the matches.

Sometimes the crowd is only around 2,000 and when the camera spans behind the goals there's hardly anybody there which isn't exactly conducive to atmosphere.

They haven't the same facilities as we have, which is hardly surprising because the game isn't yet as big over there. I remember one amusing situation in a game at the St George's Stadium in Sydney when my team Sydney Olympic played West Adelaide.

We sat on our chairs on the touchline, for there were no dug-outs as we know them. And a cameraman, with the help of two of his colleagues, kept running up and down the line with a huge camera on his shoulders, with the cable going everywhere along the line! I thought to myself: that would raise a few eyebrows at home on some of our big grounds!

But there are grounds in Australia where there are good camera angles, and there is a top-notch commentator called David Fordham who is the No. 1 man at his job on the Philips League fixture list.

So other countries have nothing to teach us with regard to our television coverage. But there are lessons we can learn from both

Australia and Germany over another increasingly important aspect of the game today – sponsorship.

The restrictions on sponsorship in Britain worry me, because they are unrealistic in this age and are administered because we have an old, stuffy and outmoded Football League system.

The League administrators are too often against progress. What I would like to see is clubs allowed to work out their own sponsorship arrangements in an unshackled way. The money is there, so why can't the clubs – particularly the less well-off – take advantage of it to the fullest extent?

Our thinking in Britain gets so muddled at times. We decide to start the 1981–82 season a fortnight later to give the clubs a bit more respite during the close season, and what's the first thing we do? Organise yet another cup competition to add to the League, the FA Cup and the League Cup!

This certainly was fodder for those who think there is too much football already, although I think this is only really true of the successful teams. If your team is a flop and doesn't do well in the cup competitions, your fixture list doesn't get cluttered up.

It's the Liverpools who get involved in too many matches, simply because they are successful, and 70 matches a season for them becomes the norm.

I'm not pessimistic about our game, far from it. I have always felt there was nothing wrong with the game, just with some of those who tamper with the laws, try to change things when they don't need changing, and so on.

For example, I don't fancy the new 1981–82 season idea of three points for a win. If they wanted to dangle an incentive to score in front of teams, what I would have liked to see is a team winning by more than three goals getting an extra point.

A team like Liverpool, who are used to winning 1-0, aren't going to change their style overnight because they are still only going to get three points for a win – a good win, a bad win or a lucky win.

The thing that appals me most about the League set-up is this annual 'old pals' act' in which teams are re-elected to the League. The same old clubs who struggle year in, year out, are duly re-elected time after time.

Altrincham should have been brought into the Football League for 1980–81 – but they failed again in 1981–82 to get in. That was out of order in my book. It hinders progress and it is a crushing blow to well-organised clubs of initiative and ambition to have their applications rejected.

They know that clubs inside who don't deserve a place in the League's framework are given the kiss of life year after year when instead they should be put out to grass.

In private enterprise, if you work hard on the understanding that there's promotion in it for you, and then suddenly at the end you are denied it, that's unfair. This is how it is with turning down deserving cases for election to the League.

When the League have allowed new clubs in from time to time, almost without exception they have done well – Shrewsbury, Cambridge United, Oxford, Hereford, Peterborough and so on.

There is every reason to suppose that a club like Altrincham, who have had a magnificent FA Cup record in recent years, would do likewise.

They are still languishing outside, however, and that sort of thing really bugs me, when I think the removal of the 'old-school tie' attitude should be first and foremost in our minds. It's almost like a form of racial discrimination!

Nobody has a divine right to League status – the Rochdales and Halifaxes have got to prove themselves and prove that they deserve it, and when they cannot, they should be put out. And that applies to any club.

When I was with Manchester United and we went down to the Second Division, I was as sick as anyone about it. I was ill. And people would say to me: 'United shouldn't be there – they're not a Second Division club.' And I would reply: 'No, we aren't – but we *are* there. And we've no divine right to be in the First Division.'

So it is with the Rochdales. If Altrincham are given their opportunity, and don't take it, fair enough – then it can be said they don't belong.

But until that happens, how can you deny them if they appear to have the necessary qualifications? And alongside some of the ailing Fourth Division clubs, they certainly do possess them.

And they talk about what they can do to improve the game? You might even do the Rochdales a favour by getting them out—it would stimulate them into greater efforts to get back.

At the moment, they virtually know they're safely in, year after year. That means they don't have to better themselves.

If a team finishes at the bottom of the Fourth Division two years running, they should automatically be out. They couldn't grumble at that because it wouldn't be a kicking-out on a 'one-off' basis.

Of course, money—or its availability—is the root problem for all clubs today more than ever before. Players' wage demands have gone through the roof and reached ridiculous proportions.

Indeed, the players have become too powerful and the tail is now wagging the dog.

I would like to see clubs paying what they can afford, and no more, on the lines of a good basic wage, with good incentives for success on top of that.

There is no fear in the players' camp today. And I think there should always be a little fear in the minds of players because it gives them an edge and means they will never be complacent. In my day, the fear of losing your place, and fear of being transferred, were always spurs.

Players no longer want a long-term contract with the security it used to provide. They now want a short, 12-month contract so that they can move on easily for bigger pickings.

The system now whereby under EEC rules a player can be valued at £1 million in Britain but can command much less—even only a quarter of that amount—on the Continent is wrong and so British clubs are not getting the true worth of a player when he is transferred. A case in point is Joe Jordan. What it boils down to is that Jordan was subsidised by Manchester United to play in Italy.

Players' agents are sprouting up all over the place. It's getting to the stage now where you're in the middle of discussing a player's contract, when he says 'Excuse me for a moment,' and scoots outside to discuss matters with his agent, then comes back in again and resumes!

My own personal view is that no player in Britain is worth £1 million. The crazy case of Steve Daley who was bought by Malcolm Allison for £1,350,000 from Wolves and later sold for about £300,000 is a classic illustration of how ridiculous it has become.

Clubs will more and more be forced to decide to carry on with what they've got and gradually the transfer ceiling will come down to manageable proportions again.

The clubs are often to blame themselves. Notts County go to Ireland and pay £100,000 for a defender. That has the effect of putting up the accepted minimum for a reasonably good player on the Irish market when it used to be something like £10,000 or £15,000. We all need to come to our senses.

I don't want the players to misunderstand me on the question of agents, and accuse me of being poacher turned gamekeeper. Even the bad players today have got agents – but I don't mind that.

I see nothing wrong in an agent working on a player's behalf commercially, as long as he doesn't poke his nose in when the manager and the player are sorting out matters like contracts, or indeed any matters within the club like training and discipline and suchlike.

We've even had agents sitting in on discussions about contracts when players are moving clubs, and doing the negotiating themselves, because some players are either shy, and afraid to ask for things themselves, or just plain dopey when it comes to matters like this.

Collectively the players are powerful today. Their union, the Professional Footballers Association, is very strong. A manager can barely sneeze today and they're appealing against it.

You can understand players wanting the proper representation, but there has to be give and take instead of all sides adopting the attitude of 'take, take'.

Perhaps the fact that 1,000 or so players have found themselves looking for a new club for the 1981-82 season will, in a way, act as a sensible brake on some of the out-of-this-world wage demands the top men are seeking.

If players are not careful, the goose will be dying long before they've got a chance to weigh the golden egg.

# 25
# A Success Down Under

ONE FACTOR above all else has given me heart in all the turbulent passages of my life, especially since I had to leave Manchester United – and that is public support.

I can say categorically that without exception, the general public have been absolutely fantastic towards me and Mary. Both at home and abroad, their attitude towards me can only be described as incredible – as if everything that has happened to me has brought them closer to me.

I get the distinct impression that they are as good as saying 'Leave the fellow alone, he's had enough.'

We've had hundreds of letters from ordinary fans wishing us well, and the whole underlying message is: 'Don't worry about it, Tom. You're a character and that's what the game lacks.'

The letters I have received since I have come back to England have been amazing. 'The game's been dead since you've been away,' was what several of them said.

It is hard for anyone to understand what a tremendous moral boost it has been to me to know the man-in-the-street, despite all my trauma, looks upon me sympathetically. No one can take that away from me.

It was exactly the same in Australia. An experience I hardly expected to face two or three years ago became one which, now it has happened to me, makes me very glad I didn't miss it.

In the shops and the restaurants down under, they'd say 'Hi, Tom – we're not reading much about Rugby Union nowadays, it's all soccer.' I felt I was wanted. I am sure I could go back tomorrow to practically any club there and name my own terms.

The spell in Australia was the first time in my life I had done a part-time job. And I think that considering all the circumstances surrounding what I set out to do with Sydney Olympic, it was the best coaching job I have ever done in my life. And to think that only a few months previously, I was feeling a little down after parting company again with QPR.

It was early autumn. I'd been given the sack, but of course in soccer, when you're a manager, you get used to that. It's certainly never depressed me for I've always found that when one door closes, another opens. But this time I knew I had the perjury case on the distant horizon, and I thought that perhaps nobody would want me until it was settled.

But within a few days the wires were humming. It seems when the Doc stops work the grapevine starts, and there's always someone who wants to use me. I had a couple of offers from Norway and one from the States.

Those Norwegian clubs clearly weren't worried about the little misunderstanding I'd had with Lillestroem precisely three years earlier in 1977. To digress for a moment, let's clear that business up for once and all.

It was a couple of months after the headlines over my United dismissal and I so fancied the idea of coaching Lillestroem that I agreed to join them for two years as coach. There was no contract ready at the time, but though I did sign an agreement to go there, I shook hands with their representative on the clear understanding that if I changed my mind between then and starting the job, they would not hold me to it.

It's history now that within a few hours, Derby County jumped in and asked me to manage them. Weighing up the two posts, I reckoned there was only one choice for me – to stay in the 'mainstream' in England.

Unfortunately the Norwegians were upset and there were even threats of suing me, but since I had not signed any contract it all died down.

I have never felt I reneged on them in view of my stipulation about changing my mind, made because I knew that in soccer things move fast and you never know what's coming around the corner.

If I have a feeling of regret now, it would have to do with fate. Perhaps had I gone through with it and taken up the Norwegian post, I might well have decided to withdraw from the Granada business, and instead of coming back to England for the case, instruct my solicitor to settle it out of court.

In addition, I would have missed that police probe episode at Derby as well, which didn't exactly boost my morale. If only I had gone to Norway...

But I stayed, and my life took a different path—the path that eventually took me across the other side of the world to Australia.

So, to get back to the story, there I was out of work, and not for the first time in my career wondering what my next move would be, when I got a call from an old friend Johnny Thompson asking me if I'd like to go to Aussie-land.

It would only be for eight months or so, he explained, until my court case came up. So Mary and I went out to Sydney for a couple of weeks to have a look at the Olympic club I was to coach. It really also meant a welcome holiday for the pair of us.

I liked the place, the money was good, and as it would serve as a very pleasant stop-gap until my court case, I said 'Okay—I'll come.' It may have been part-time, but it was hard work and I needed to throw myself into the job because of the raw material I had at my disposal and the standard of the players.

At the end, I looked back and I was pretty satisfied with what I'd achieved. Australian soccer will get better, of that I'm sure. The standard of their top teams is roughly equivalent to British Third and Fourth Division teams.

Olympic weren't only learning from me—I was also learning, because I had to gear my schedule to a part-time basis for the first time in my life.

We trained three nights a week and played our matches on Sundays. But because of the direct involvement I and other coaches had with the media out there it meant a fairly full week.

As part of my contract with the club, I had to do a column for the Australian *Soccer Weekly*. In addition, I was doing a regular piece for both the *Sydney Morning Herald* and the *Sydney Sun*, and on top of that I found myself a regular spot on a TV sports programme called Channel O with people like David Fordham, one of the top sports personalities who knows the Australian game inside out, Peter Skelton, Alec Henderson, John Rowley, and Hugh Johns, well known in Britain as a commentator for ITV.

Every Friday after the programme was over we would pop across the road to a marvellous French restaurant called Wilsons, have a nice lunch and a drink or two with any of the celebrities who had been on the air with us.

They included Brian Lefair, secretary of the Australian Soccer Federation, Paul Kemp, the secretary of the League and equivalent to Graham Kelly in England, and Sir Arthur George, the Federation president.

All this togetherness, which I felt was very good for the game – the constant swopping of opinion and views – was somewhat tarnished by a report which appeared after I had returned to England and which said that I had slated Australian soccer.

This was totally unfounded. I couldn't have done a thing like that, because Australian football was good to me and I was grateful to the folk out there for giving me the chance to extend my experience. From every club I went to for an away game, I received a marvellous personal reception. They told me that they felt I was bringing something valuable into the Australian game.

So I was annoyed and alarmed when I read this report which I thought would be misconstrued down under and might give the impression that I was biting the hand which had fed me.

I think the misunderstanding arose after a team called Footscray had come to our ground and played ultra-defensively. It was a bit pathetic and at the time they were drawing only about 400 people to watch their home matches. I made a comment in the Australian Press that if this was the way they played, I could understand why so few people wanted to watch them.

That was in no way a general condemnation of Australian soccer, for which I have every admiration. Aussies work hard at the game, and in the end they are bound to succeed.

Indeed, I would go so far as to say that the game will eventually be bigger and better than it is in the United States. Reasons? For one thing, Australians base a lot of their thinking on the British and European game, and many of the people involved in playing, coaching and managing are from Europe.

Second the weather is great so the game can be played literally all the year round. Everything is set fair for an impact.

So I would never denigrate the Australian game. Of course, if I could criticise constructively any aspect of it in my efforts to help it along, then naturally I would.

There seems to be no animosity between the clubs–only healthy rivalry. The people who ran clubs like Marconi and Hakoah used to have a little meeting every week to discuss the various problems which had arisen and how they could be tackled.

That would never happen in Britain because of the sheer size of the game, and also the jealousies between clubs.

The way they allow sponsorship to have a free rein in Australia does only good for the game. If people want to put money into soccer, why find ways and means to block them? This is one of the reasons why the game in Britain is struggling financially. Our natural reserve seems to put the brake on anything new, even if it is obviously a good idea.

Australian soccer is 'down the league' when it comes to spectator sport. The very fact that it has to compete alongside its big brothers–Rugby League, Rugby Union, Australian rules football and the cricket gives it an edge. It has to be alert to make headway.

If I hadn't landed the Preston North End job, I would almost certainly have gone back out to Australia after the court case, and probably stayed for four or five years.

As it stands now, I shall return there once a year for four or five weeks–that's how much I liked being there.

If I had landed the national manager's job there, I would probably have stayed. There was considerable talk that it might come my way, but it didn't.

There was a lot of disappointment about Australia's failure even to qualify for a play-off in their World Cup group for the 1982 finals, particularly after their magnificent effort in reaching the 1974 finals in Munich.

They still don't have a national soccer stadium–so there's a way to go yet. They've had mixed luck with their various coaches. Nevertheless, I'm convinced the breakthrough will come, because they play soccer as we in Britain know it—and that's the best. There are no gimmicks as there are in the States—awful things like shoot-outs and all the razzmatazz before the game. That's the American way.

Philips, the big electrical firm, sponsor the League, which is just as well because travelling, as you might imagine, is very expensive with the gigantic distances involved compared with those between British clubs.

This brings me back once again to the vexed question of sponsorship and the extraordinary fact that to a large extent in Britain, it is still almost a dirty word.

If the game reached a stage in Britain where it might be dying—which for all our sakes, I hope it never will be—and only sponsorship would keep it alive, then maybe we'd change our archaic attitude towards it.

Frankly, if I were in charge of a club like Liverpool or Manchester United, I would just go my own way in this respect and do what Jim Gregory has done at QPR with the astro-turf pitch.

I appreciate that this venture will give both QPR and their opponents a few problems. But it will also bring QPR a lot of revenue, and I think you'll find that the entertainment at Shepherd's Bush could extend to boxing, with matchmakers like Micky Duff being very much involved.

That's the sort of thing they do in Australia—different sports in the same stadium. Jim Gregory has the foresight to try it out here—good luck to him.

While I was in Australia and wondering what the future held for me either there or back home, I had a chance to view the British game from a distance, which gave me a different sort of insight into it from that I had when wrapped up in it day by day.

And in a peculiar sort of way, it gave me fresh hope when I came to the conclusion that the managerial merry-go-round back home seemed to be a game of 'sack one flop, take on another.' Consider some of the examples.

Alan Durban, who hadn't done anything world-shattering at

Stoke, went to Sunderland. And Richie Barker, No. 2 at Wolves, who haven't broken any pots and pans in recent years, took his place.

Alan Ball was a complete flop at Blackpool and has been succeeded by Allan Brown, whom Blackpool had sacked when he was in the job before. Gordon Milne, a nice guy who worked damned hard at Coventry but didn't win anything, has been kicked upstairs and replaced by Dave Sexton, who did not set the world on fire at Manchester United.

Terry Venables, who left Crystal Palace floundering at the foot of the First Division, went to QPR. John Neal, who couldn't pull up any trees at Middlesbrough, has gone to Chelsea to take over from Geoff Hurst, who was fired from Stamford Bridge.

Ronnie Allen, who left West Bromwich Albion previously, and didn't exactly set the world alight in Greece, has got his old job back again.

So it seemed to me that the qualification to get a job in England was that you had to be something of a failure!

Clubs are engaging new managers just because they provide a fresh face, not necessarily because they've got good track records at the clubs they've left.

So I had absolutely no qualms about saying goodbye to Australia and coming back to try to revive Preston's fortunes. Returning to Deepdale was like coming back home—as if I'd done the full circle.

Not long after I arrived back, I walked into the dressing-room—and there in front of me was the exact peg where I'd first hung my shirt way back in 1949!

A lot of water has flowed under the bridge since then. I fancy if you'd told me then—32 years ago—what would befall me in the following years, it would have frightened me to death!

It is strange and pleasant, returning to be manager at the club where such a great player as Tom Finney appeared with me, and where he is now the club president.

Preston are ambitious—and so am I, even at this stage of my life. Who knows, in four or five years time I may be tired of it all. But until such time, the old fires still burn . . .

# 26
# Quotes Along the Way

WHAT THEY SAID ABOUT ME ...

*TOM FINNEY* (after the 1954 Preston-West Bromwich FA Cup Final): This player is going to make a great manager one day although he takes a lot of understanding. But wherever he goes and whatever he does, they will certainly know he has been there.

*ROD STEWART:* I would come back to live in England if the Doc were Prime Minister.

*PAT CRERAND:* As an enemy, Doc was vicious, vindictive and callous.

*JIM GREGORY* (QPR chairman): If Doc had been a car salesman, he'd have made a million pounds.

*ERIC PURSHOUSE* (Rotherham chairman): If I had to spend 10 years in gaol and had to choose a companion, I'd choose Doc. He'd make it seem like one year.

*TOMMY CAVANAGH:* He eats cheats for breakfast. He's the only manager I know who can hold a serious, face-to-face conversation and tell you what's happening twenty yards behind him.

*SYD GRAY* (my Army CO in Palestine): Tommy was my platoon sergeant. He was one helluva soldier—not some rumbustious hell-raiser—just a quiet, dependable, efficient guy you could count on to do what was right when the chips were down.

*NOEL CANTWELL* (after I was sacked at Villa): Tommy is a sad loss to the game. He is one of soccer's great characters and it can ill afford to have him on the sidelines.

*GERRY DALY:* The Doc and I couldn't stand each other.

*TOM FINNEY* (on my return to Preston): Doc is never at a loss for words and no one can ever hurt him.

*NEVILLE BRIGGS* (chief scout, Stoke City): Whenever people criticise Tommy to my face I ask them if they either know him or have worked with him. When they say no my reply is 'All you know is what you read in the newspapers—he is the finest bloke I've ever worked with in the game'.

## WHAT I SAID ABOUT THEM ...

I told the Chelsea chairman he didn't want a coach—he needed a hearse.

I promised Rotherham I'd take them out of the Second Division. I did—into the Third Division.

There's a hell of a lot of politics in football. I don't think Henry Kissinger would have lasted 48 hours at Old Trafford.

Jim Gregory was a man of whims—one day he'd be very generous and give you anything. The next day his mood could change—and if he was a ghost, he wouldn't give you a fright.

I've had more clubs than Jack Nicklaus.

You could be with Dave Sexton a year and never get to know him.

Billy Bremner was a great player—probably better than me—because he was better coached.

When Doug Ellis told me he and the Villa board had given me a vote of confidence, I said I'd better go home and pack my bags because that was a sure sign I was about to get the bullet.

I think I've been in more courts than Bjorn Borg.

# THE DOCHERTY DATELINE

Glasgow Celtic       *August 1947*

Preston North End    *November 1949*

Arsenal              *August 1958*

Chelsea              *February 1961*

COACH/MANAGER

Chelsea              *February 1961 coach*
                     *January 1962 manager*
                     *October 1967 resigned*

Rotherham Utd        *November 1967 manager*
                     *November 1968 resigned*

Queen's Park Rangers  *November 1968 manager*
                      *December 1968 resigned*

Aston Villa          *December 1968 manager*
                     *January 1970 sacked*

Oporto               *February 1970 coach*
                     *May 1971 end of contractual period*

Hull City            *July 1971 assistant manager*
                     *November 1971 left by mutual consent*

Scotland             *September 1971 caretaker-manager*
                     *November 1971 manager*
                     *December 1972 resigned*

Manchester United    *December 1972 manager*
                     *July 1977 sacked*

Derby County         *September 1977 manager*
                     *April 1979 resigned*

Queen's Park Rangers  *May 1979 manager*
                      *October 1980 sacked*

Sydney Olympic       *October 1980 coach*
                     *June 1981 left by mutual consent*

Preston North End    *June 1981 manager*